DON'T WEAR

Flip-Flops

TO YOUR

Interview

DON'T WEAR
Flip-Flops
TO YOUR
Interview

And Other Obvious Tips That You Should Be Following to Get the Job *You Want*

DR. PAUL POWERS

CAREER PRESS The Career Press, Inc.
Wayne, N.J.

DON'T WEAR FLIP-FLOPS TO YOUR INTERVIEW
EDITED AND TYPESET BY KARA KUMPEL
Cover design by Rob Johnson/Toprotype
Printed in the U.S.A.
Previously published as *Winning Job Interviews*

To order this title, please call toll-free 1-800-CAREER-1 (NJ and Canada: 201-848-0310) to order using VISA or MasterCard, or for further information on books from Career Press.

CAREER
PRESS

The Career Press, Inc.
12 Parish Drive
Wayne, NJ
www.careerpress.com

Library of Congress Cataloging-in-Publication Data
Powers, Paul (Management psychologist)
  Don't wear flip-flops to your interview : and other obvious tips that you should be following to get the job you want / by Dr. Paul Powers.
      pages cm
  Includes index.
  ISBN 978-1-63265-003-0 -- ISBN 978-1-63265-996-5 (ebook)
  1. Employment interviewing. 2. Job hunting. I. Title.

HF5549.5.I6P687 2015
650.14'4--dc23

                                        2015008947

For Linda.

For your unreserved support, sustaining confidence,
and abundant love.

Contents

Introduction

IF YOU JUST PICKED UP THIS BOOK IT'S BECAUSE YOU WANT OR ARE THINKING ABOUT OR NEED A NEW JOB. Good for you! Let me ask you why. Do you sense there is something better for you out there? Good. Do you want a job that engages more of your brainpower and personality, more of your talents, more of your life energy? Good. Do you want a job that pays you more money? Good. Do you want a job that moves you ever closer to your life goals? Good. This book is the shortest distance between you and that job.

I have written this book so you can get through it in just a couple of sessions in order for you to crank up your job search more quickly. As you can already tell from this introduction I use a very conversational tone, as if it were just you and I talking together. That is to keep you engaged and moving forward—ever forward. No putting it down and thinking, *Maybe I'll get back to it later.* To heck with that. What I uncovered for you in the first paragraph on this page is a bit of your discontent—and that's a good thing. Tap into it. Use it. If you want something better, go for it. It's all up to you, because the job fairy isn't coming for you today, tomorrow, or ever.

Between these two covers are 30-plus years of my professional experience as a career expert, organizational psychologist, and author. You'll find market-proven techniques, new approaches, and shortcuts around the roadblocks that will stymie most job hunters. I've included several diagrams to quickly reinforce major points I make in the text. When you see one of these diagrams, do not skim over it because it's there to emphasize something your competitors often miss. Another bonus is The Good to Great Interview Toolkit contained in Chapter 10 that will support you and keep you on track at every step of the process.

The job-hunting process in general, and job interviewing in particular, requires focus, energy, optimism, and a sense of humor. In the pages of this book you will find liberal doses of each. You won't find a lot of extraneous material to distract you from what you really need to know about job-hunting and interviewing success.

In workshops and seminars, at conferences and conventions all over the country, in one-on-one counseling or coaching sessions, or just hanging out in the break room or cafeteria, scores of people have honored me with the stories of their work lives—their hopes, their dreams, their fears, their failures. Once upon a time, the best employers were willing and mostly able to look out for and support their employees' jobs and careers in a paternalistic and caring way. In rare environments a few vestigial pockets of that attitude remain today, but, by and large, that world is gone—and gone forever. At the 30-year mark in my profession, I believe, now more fervently than ever before, that every individual must learn the skills to manage and advance his or her own career, and that you, truly, must be the captain of your own fate, because nobody else is out there looking out for you.

If you put to work what is in this short but powerful book, you will be ready to either maximize your opportunities in a booming economy or survive any recession and come out on top. That's what I call packing your own parachute, and in either circumstance, you should start today.

Career management, job hunting, making a living, and job interviewing are all serious issues. Serious? Yes. Solemn? No. None of us gets out of this life alive, my friend, and I've learned that a good laugh can help us endure and succeed in even the most difficult circumstances. Thus, throughout this book, my little quips, humorous asides, and optimistic observations are meant to help you keep this whole process in its proper perspective.

If you want a career book that will put you to sleep and collude with you to postpone your actual job-hunting for another day with theories, case studies, research studies, meditations, and other extraneous material (and there are plenty of them out there), you'll have to look elsewhere. If you want to hit the ground running with all the knowledge, insider tips, and tools you need right at your fingertips, you're holding the right book.

So, enough of the pep talk. Let's get down to work.

Chapter 1

Job Hunting Does *Not* Have to Suck

EVERY JOB HUNTER HAS A HORROR STORY TO TELL. So does every athlete, every musician, every hairdresser, every boater, every artist, every plumber, and every golfer. Name any human endeavor and there is someone somewhere who can tell you something ugly that happened while engaging in that activity. But the occasional adversity *does not define* that activity (except for, perhaps, my golf game). Mistakes, gaffes, and setbacks are all part and parcel of any process requiring skill. Job hunting is no exception. But obstacles and impediments can be minimized (and often completely avoided) by learning from the mistakes of those who have gone before you and from recognizing and correcting the mistakes you make on your own. It is for this reason that I have written this book for you.

Yes, job hunting can suck. But it doesn't *have* to. By taking the time and energy to dissect and understand the process, learn from the experiences of others, identify the skills you need, and have the guts to assess and learn from your own performance along the way, you can go from being a good job hunter to a great job hunter.

Yes, you will encounter obstacles on your path to a new job. If you use all that this book has to offer, I promise that your path will be smoother, shorter, and sometimes even a little fun. I wrote it so that you can read it in one weekend or a couple of nights. But reading it is not enough; you must put this stuff to work. You've got to try out some new behaviors. Today's competition for jobs is tougher than ever before, and what worked for you in the past may not work now, so you need to work both harder and smarter. But first you need to know what you are up against.

If I were writing this book for other psychologists, career coaches, or outplacement experts, I would have called this chapter "How to Identify and Resolve the Negative Psychosocial Consequences Experienced by Individuals in the Employment Transition Process." Not a bad title for a master's thesis or doctoral dissertation. But I'm writing this book for you, the job hunter, who needs solid input that is market-proven, quickly usable, and with no punches pulled.

Though the job interview is the single most important element of the job-changing process, it is critical for you to remember that it is only one part—paramount though it may be—of that entire *process*. And for you to succeed—to win—in these critical interview situations, you must have a firm, realistic understanding of the entire job-hunting process. Armed with the knowledge in this book, you will be able to control the process, not be controlled by it; you will be able to drive the process rather than be driven crazy by it.

People who have recently completed the job-hunting process will tell you that it is one of the hardest things they ever had to do. Sure, there is the occasional lucky person who has a new job fall in his or her lap—sports stars, former politicians, media figures. Good for them; but it has never happened to me, and I bet it has never happened to you. For the rest of us ordinary schnooks, job hunting is hard work. But now, finally, for some good news: the hard work that you invest in your job hunt will pay off in positive ways like almost nothing else.

The rewards for fully engaging one's self in this demanding job-hunting process are many. You can find a team of people with whom you enjoy working, you can find a boss you respect, you can add to your social circle, you can find colleagues or mentors from whom you can learn, you may actually make more money and, best of all, you can discover work that has personal meaning for you beyond a mere paycheck. You will feel more professionally accomplished and more personally competent. You will have more energy and vitality that you can then share with those closest to you, and, thus, you will receive more from them in return. You will be building a continuously reinforcing cycle of achievement and success in multiple areas of your life.

This all sounds terrific, but if this process can bring such wonderful rewards, why do the vast majority of job hunters hate it so much? The answer is that there is a predictable series of psychological stumbling blocks that can trip up even the most determined job hunter.

The Top 10 Roadblocks to Successful Job Hunting

From more than 30 years of working in different aspects of the career field, I have identified 10 major psychological roadblocks that can sidetrack, confuse, and discourage even the most dedicated the job hunter. These roadblocks are both powerful and insidious; they are at work even when you're not aware of them. They are among the most compelling reasons that many people stay in a dead-end job or try to avoid the job-hunting process at all costs—to the detriment of both their career and overall quality of life.

If you are going to be a successful job hunter (and this, in no small part, means becoming a great job interviewer), you will need to recognize, face up to, and overcome each of these factors. By getting these roadblocks out in the open and learning how to get around them, you will automatically put yourself in the top tier of smart job hunters. With my help you can do it, so let's get started.

1. Starting Without a Crisp, Clear, Realistic Goal

Many job hunters/job interviewers start the process by making a few phone calls looking for leads or scanning online job banks/job listings. When this initial effort fails to turn up something wonderful in a relatively short period of time (as often it does), the typical job hunter starts to get discouraged. You hear them say, "We're in a bad job market these days," "There's nothing much available in my field right now," "This isn't a good time of the year to be looking," "I'll keep you mind," and so on.

He or she then begins to put in even less effort and, predictably, gets even fewer if any positive results. Soon this becomes a self-reinforcing cycle of defeat. It overwhelms the job hunter and convinces him that maybe it's best to just hang onto the mediocre job he has now or settle for something that's easy to find or that may be beneath what he is capable of. This is roadblock number one at its worst.

The first step in any successful job search is to develop a clear, crisp, realistic goal. If you can't describe what kind of job you are looking for in one or two sentences, you are not ready to be out there in the job market asking for interviews.

You must be ready to state clearly what type of position you are looking for, in what type of organization, and in what geographic area, and you must be able to make a persuasive case based upon your knowledge, your skills, your experience, and your personal characteristics as to why someone should hire you to do this job for a reasonable salary. If you are not armed with this information, you are going to waste a lot of time and energy spinning your wheels and pursuing targets that are inappropriate or not worth your effort.

You must overcome this roadblock before you attempt to move your job search into high gear. If you know exactly what you're looking for, where to look for it, and how best to find it—great! But if you are not sure you're fully ready to conduct a professional, fine-tuned, multi-front job campaign, turn to The Good to Great Interview Toolkit in Chapter 10 and get to work on Tool #1: Job Hunt Readiness Assessment.

Note that the job you ultimately land may not be the one you started out looking for. There are all sorts of reasons that this might be the case, such as technology changes, marketplace disruptions, and new positions being created from merging or eliminating old ones. The essential point here is not to embark on a rigorous process with a wishy-washy "I don't know what I want" or "I'm wondering what is out there" attitude. To attract the attention you want, you need to sound thoughtful, self-assured, and focused.

2. No Control Over the Timing of the Job Hunt

Very few folks take the effort to assess the job market when things are going great. You should do this, of course, but that is a discussion for another day. Job hunting requires such energy and focus that most folks wait until something beyond their control forces them to make a move. Maybe it's a reduction in force (RIF), a layoff, a plant closing, a merger, a product recall, a boss bringing in his own team, or jobs being sent overseas that provides the motivation. Maybe you saw the writing on the wall but didn't have time to jump before you were pushed. If this hasn't yet happened to you in your career, stay tuned, because one day it surely will. The reality is that very few of us take the bull by the horns and get an aggressive, professional job search underway before we are told that we have to.

Despite the initial discomfort that comes with any of these scenarios, it is actually one of those "good news/bad news" things. The bad news is obvious. The vast majority of job hunters are thrown into a process that makes great demands on them for energy, creativity, and productivity all while playing "beat the clock" with their incoming severance pay or unemployment compensation and (God willing) their savings on one hand, and their outgoing cash flow, rent/mortgage, and bills on the other. It's no small wonder that many job hunters get down in the dumps.

If you are resentful that you have to job hunt at a time not of your own choosing, you must address this issue and get it out of the way. Use your employee assistance program, outplacement consultant, and career or unemployment counselor to advise you. Locate and join a job search networking/support group. If you are finding it impossible to concentrate on your job hunt because you are constantly obsessing or worried about money, sharpen your pencil and work out a realistic budget for a job hunt with a realistic timeline.

Don't try to ignore this feeling, because it will surface when you want it least. Some anxiety is normal and predictable in any job search, but if it grows into panic, it can affect your behavior as well as your attitude. You may expect things to happen too quickly, and not reaching these unrealistic goals will create more anxiety. It will push you to look and sound desperate, and this is the demise of any job interview. It will impair your vision so that you may see the first job that pops up, perhaps one that's only so-so, as a good job that you should take. In Chapter 2, I'll show you how to control your anxiety at every phase of the interviewing and job-hunting process.

You're probably asking, "Okay, Paul, so what's the good news already?" Well, the good news is that you are completely free to actively and professionally pursue the job of your dreams on a full-time basis. You are not limited to job hunting on your lunch hour or when the boss isn't around. You no longer have to sneak off to interviews during phony dentist appointments. You don't have to worry about having someone overhearing you on the phone or looking over your shoulder while you're on your computer. You can freely ask your current colleagues for their input, advice, and networking contacts. You can ask your human resources person for referrals to employment agencies. All of these actions will help you succeed in your job hunt—and more quickly than if you had to do it on an on-the-sly, part-time basis.

This is in no way meant to suggest that you ignore the fact that your financial situation may be somewhat precarious, or that you shouldn't demand more thought, a tighter budget, or perhaps some alternative arrangements such as temping, part-time work, consulting, and so on. I merely want to reinforce for you that thousands and thousands of job hunters have somehow scraped by financially *and* found great jobs at a time not of their choosing. You can, too.

3. It's All About Rejection, Baby

There are very few people in life who thrive on rejection. Salespeople have learned how to do it and the most successful salespeople I've ever met seem to be built in a psychologically different way from the rest of us. Saying no to a good salesperson is not like saying no to the rest of us. To them, a no means "not yet" or "you haven't told me enough" or "maybe later" or "we need to negotiate" about price, timing, or something else. A successful salesperson doesn't take the first, second, or even third no as a bona fide rejection. (By the way, this is one of the reasons that salespeople make such effective job hunters.)

But how many of the rest of us really thrive on rejection? I don't; do you? *The job-hunting process is essentially a series of rejections* with an occasional piece of good news thrown in just to keep you from sticking your head in the oven. Right now, read the italicized part of the previous sentence out loud three times; it's really important that you absorb it. Your spouse, partner, roommate, cat, or dog might think you're a little crazy, but why not give 'em a taste now of what's to come?

Here's what the typical job hunt looks like. Time after time you go through the process of uncovering a job lead through whatever method you used that day. You chase down this lead with a resume, following up with a letter, e-mail, and/or a series of phone calls, working your way through a series of interviews, sending out the thank-you letters or e-mails, and getting your hopes up, all for the statistical likelihood of not getting the job. Sounds fun, eh? Sure—like banging your head against the wall; it only feels good when you stop!

Realistically, you will probably go through this process a number of times before the job you really want comes through. Another unfortunate reality—but a reality that must be faced nonetheless—is that the job-hunting process contains a whole lot more rejection than acceptance.

The biggest key to overcoming this roadblock is for you to understand that *this is the essential nature of the process.* Getting rejected doesn't mean that you're doing it wrong; it means that you're doing it right! In fact, I tell job hunters that if they aren't getting rejected a lot, either they aren't job hunting hard enough or they aren't searching for a job that represents a step forward for them.

Another way to overcome this sense of rejection is to realize that the employer didn't make a negative decision about hiring you. This is not just a case of semantics. What has happened is no longer about you. What has happened is that the employer made a positive decision to hire somebody else. Obviously, that person made a better case—looked like a better fit—than you did. Try to come up with some ideas as to how you could have presented yourself in a stronger light and try those techniques during your next interview. Put this hard-won information to work for you by including it in your post-interview notes. (Tool #14: Post-Interview Evaluation and Improvement in Chapter 10 will be a great help here.) Remember, this is a learning process. You can and will get better at it with time if you work at it.

There is another important point to remember that may surprise you, given my typically low assessment of the interviewing skills of those who will be evaluating you. (And this is constantly bolstered by reports to me from hundreds of job hunters just like you.) There are some interviewers (a minority, I admit) who are really good at matching job candidates to the right job. If you are fortunate enough to be interviewed by one of these rare experts but, unfortunately, are rejected for the position in question, maybe you should breathe a sigh of relief. There is something worse than not getting a job you hoped for—and that is *getting* a job you're unsuited for and in which you will ultimately fail.

Lastly, don't be paranoid. No one has so little to do or so much time on their hands that they are out there interviewing people just to sadistically reject them. I'm sorry to say it may feel that way sometimes, but it's just not so.

4. It's Unpredictable

By and large, human beings don't like surprises. I know that I don't. Okay, maybe I like that rare piece of unexpected good news or a real letter from a friend, or a thoughtful thank you. But I'm willing to bet that people in funny hats jumping out of dark closets yelling "SURPRISE!" are responsible for as many heart attacks as cheeseburgers. When the phone or doorbell rings late at night, I'm under no illusion that it's the Publisher's Clearing House prize patrol!

This, most likely, goes back to our caveman past when a big, exciting surprise was apt to be something such as an 800-pound, snarling saber-toothed tiger about to rip the head from your shoulders. Surprises were usually bad news. (Think about this the next time you're crouching in the dark in somebody's front hall closet with their raincoats and umbrellas.) To heck with surprises; give me predictability.

Well, guess what? The job-hunting process is totally unpredictable except for one thing: if you work hard at it, you *will* eventually get a job. And this one certainty is one that you will have to take from me on faith. And though you may believe this intellectually, there will be discouraging days during your job hunt when it will *feel like* you'll never get a job.

Let's take a look at all the uncertainties of the job search. You do not know how long your job search will take. You do not know the name of the organization in which you will end up working. You do not know the specific job you will end up doing. You do not know who will be your boss. You don't know where this organization will be located. You don't know who your peers will be. You may not know the industry your employer will be in. You do not know the details of your salary and benefits. With all these uncertainties, it is only natural to be apprehensive about the job-hunting process.

One caller to my *CareerTalk* radio show said it best: "Being a job hunter is worse than being a convict in prison. A convict at least knows when he is eligible for parole so he can make some plans for the future. But a job hunter is more like a hostage because there is no set date to pin one's hopes on. You just have to tough it out day by day and keep the faith that something good will eventually happen." This is a pretty stark analogy, but there is wisdom in it. If you work hard at your search *and* you keep the faith that something good will happen, it will. I just can't predict when. Sorry 'bout that.

5. It Lacks Structure

In one of my earlier books, *Love Your Job!* I identify many of the benefits of having a great job. Heck, one of the benefits of even a so-so job is that it provides structure to your everyday life.

For most of us, structure is comfortable; it's knowing what time to get up in the morning, knowing the route or method of your commute, knowing who you will be working with, having a basic understanding of the types of challenges you will face during the day, knowing (perhaps praying for) the time that you will be done for the day, and knowing what time you need to go to bed to get enough rest to do it all over again tomorrow.

The job hunt does not provide this kind of structure. The amount of time you spend on any particular job hunting technique is up to you. The sequence in which you tackle tasks is completely up to you. The amount of energy and drive you put into your search is all up to you. The time of day you start and the time of day you stop working is all up to you. Who you will see or will not see is up to you. You are now running a completely independent operation.

To some folks, this independence is exhilarating. It's like running your own business. If this is your experience, it may be a good indicator that you should ultimately be your own boss. (Whether or not this is the best time to do that is an entirely different issue.)

To many people, the job hunt feels like being cut adrift, alone, in a small boat, with no idea in which direction to row in order to get safely home. If you thrive on this degree of self-direction, you are fortunate. If you don't, don't beat yourself up over it. The majority of the world feels the way that you do. Here's how you deal with it.

If you found yourself on a desert island with nothing to protect you from the wind and rain, what would you do? Think back to Tom Hanks in the movie *Castaway.* Obviously, you would build a shelter. It might not be perfect at first, but with time you would improve this structure, making it more secure, stronger, and more comfortable. You wouldn't build a bigger structure than you needed. Nor would you build one that wouldn't meet your needs. This is what you must do during your job search—build a structure that meets your needs.

You must force yourself to answer such questions as: What time will I start on my job search each morning? What are my weekly goals?

What are my monthly goals? When do I predict I will be re-employed? When will I go to the library, or how much time will I spend online to do my research? How much time will I devote to networking? How many sources of published openings will I review weekly? How many employment agency/search firm contacts are enough? How much time should I spend on the telephone? You must recognize that you are now self-employed and the only person who can answer these questions is you.

The only structure you will find in the job-hunting process is that which you provide for yourself. If you need it, it only makes sense to build it for yourself and come in out of the rain. (Tool #4 in the Toolkit, Job Hunt Goal-Setting and Monitoring, will help you set, customize, and reach your weekly and monthly job search goals.)

6. G.r.r.s

No, I'm not referring to the guttural sound coming from the back of your throat when someone who you thought would be great help to you blows you off or you don't get a job you wanted or any one of the many things that will aggravate you during the job-hunting process. G.r.r. is my acronym for gender-related roadblock. Both men and women encounter most job-hunting obstacles in about equal proportion. But in my decades of experience, I have seen two that are experienced by a significantly higher percentage by either male or female job hunters. Let's take a look.

Job Hunting Requires Asking for Help

Both men and women stumbled over this roadblock, but I have observed a much higher percentage of men struggling with this one. Let's use an example most of us can relate to. Have you ever noticed a person continually driving around and around the same block, craning his neck looking for street numbers or landmarks, swerving from one side of the road to the other while frantically glancing down at a scrap of paper held in one hand? What's going on here?

You guessed it—he's lost. Now, whereas some of us would prefer to use such terms as "momentarily disoriented," "geographically impaired," or "temporarily uncertain as to my *exact* position," this guy needs help. Why is it that some people would rather struggle along with a problem by themselves than to ask for help from others?

Some have suggested that men have this problem because of sex-role stereotypes, as in, "I'm a manly man; I don't *need* help, I *give* help!" This is probably true to some extent, but it doesn't explain why some women also labor needlessly in this regard. Perhaps it has less to do with gender (nature) and more to do with the degree of independence we were accustomed to in our environment as we grew up (nurture). Whatever the reason for this attitude, it is counterproductive to your job-hunting success and it will make the process both longer and more difficult.

If you have this "I must do it on my own" attitude, you've got to overcome it. To help you do this, I have compiled "Dr. Paul's Short Course on Humility." To complete this course, read the following statements and respond with a true or false.

- ➤ I know exactly what types of jobs are available in my geographical area and occupational field.   True   False

- ➤ I know precisely the salary ranges and benefits that these jobs provide.   True   False

- ➤ I know every source of published openings and help-wanted ads in print and online for people in my field.   True   False

- ➤ I know of and can speak to all employment agencies and search firms that work in my field.   True   False

- ➤ I am confident that my resume and my letters are the best they can be.   True   False

- ➤ I am completely familiar with all the libraries, schools, colleges, Websites, and public offices that have relevant information I will need during my job search.   True   False

- ➤ Secretaries and administrative assistants swoon at the mere sound of my voice and always put my phone calls through on my first try.   True   False

- ➤ I have a personal network of between 100 and 200 people who will be willing to help me with my job search. And I know how to get them to help me.   True   False

- ➤ I love making telephone calls to people I don't know.   True   False

➹ When faced with rejection, I never get
discouraged.   True   False

➹ When faced with a hard, frustrating task, I find
that isolation and lack of brainstorming helps
me to become more creative.   True   False

If you answered false to *any* of the previous items, you need help. This is not a weakness; it is an essential element of the job-hunting game. Whenever you are tempted to tough it out alone, remember Dr. Paul's short course on humility. Humility means putting your pride in your pocket. And by doing that, I guarantee a paycheck will soon follow.

Job Hunting Requires Tooting One's Own Horn

If it seems like I've been picking on men, the tables are about to turn. Another reason job hunting seems so difficult is that you have to blow your own horn. Many people (and here I have found a higher percentage of women) have a hard time selling themselves. Many of us (men as well as women) were taught that it was not polite or seemly to talk about ourselves: all the wonderful things we have accomplished, or the kudos we've received, or all the insightful thoughts we have, or the many terrific personal characteristics that we have developed. I have observed that many female job hunters are better at sharing credit with others and detailing collaborative efforts than some men. I think this is a strong selling point as long as it doesn't come at the expense of highlighting one's own contributions and accomplishments.

One frustrated job hunter once said to me, "I hate this. I'm a back office type. If I wanted to be a salesperson, I would have *become one.*" My response was, "You are a job hunter, which means you've just been transferred to the sales department. Welcome aboard!"

To overcome this hesitancy to sell yourself, you will need practice, coaching, and feedback. By the way, this is how good salespeople become great salespeople. When you talk to a close contact about your job search, ask him or her if you came on too strong or if it would be better to come on a little stronger. When you meet recruiters, ask them for feedback about your personal presentation. If you discover important accomplishments that you've neglected to put on your resume, be sure to revise it to include them. If, after some of your preliminary interviews, you feel comfortable with an interviewer, ask him or her for some feedback about your style. If you get feedback that you are too laid back, then it may help you to take an assertiveness training workshop.

No prospective employer looks at the hiring process as a detective job or a hidden-treasure hunt. They will only learn as much about you as *you* are willing to share. The more data you put on the table about yourself, as it relates to this employment opportunity, the better chance you stand of getting the job offer you want. It's that simple. If you sit there waiting and hoping to be discovered, like a starlet in some 1940s movie, you will fail.

7. It's Lonely and Isolating

To the unemployed job hunter, it looks like everybody else in the entire world has a job. People driving down your street during the morning commute seem clearly different from you. They have someplace that they have to be, where there are people with whom they have to meet. You, on the other hand, are on your own to figure out for yourself what it is that you have to do. During off hours, many job hunters feel that their friends and family do not want to hear about their job search because somehow it reflects negatively on them that they are unemployed. And after all, who wants to be continually giving the bad news that, "No, I haven't found a job yet."

If you are gainfully employed while looking for a job, it can be even lonelier because, realistically, there are very few people at work with whom you should risk discussing your job search. I have observed that the best bosses, those interested in their employees' growth and career development, are quite willing to have their employees know what their career options are in the open job market. However, not all bosses are that secure, and most folks have good reason to fear that their boss will hear through the grapevine (as Marvin Gaye would say) that they are actively looking for a new job.

These and other factors combine to make the job-hunting process a lonely and isolating experience. The problem is that loneliness and isolation are the mortal enemies of high energy and a positive attitude, both of which you will need to succeed as a job hunter. The way to overcome this roadblock is to learn that you cannot succeed at this process by yourself; you will need other people.

If you are looking for a job while unemployed, there are a number of ways to connect with other job hunters who can keep you from becoming lonely and isolated. If you have outplacement assistance, be sure to avail yourself of the group meetings and networking forums that the out-placement firm provides. Most state unemployment or employment and training offices offer networking support groups. Many community and church groups now either sponsor job search networking groups or let them use their facilities. Get involved in these groups, maybe even help to run one, and you will be amazed at how helpful they will be; to help you generate leads, to help you keep focused, and to help keep you con-nected with other people.

If you are looking for a job while employed and don't want to join a public networking group, you will have to construct one of your own. From talking with your associates at work, friends and family, and from a larger range of contacts, you could probably identify four to six people who are looking for a new job at any one time. Try to organize reg-ular group meetings. Or, if that is impossible, try discussing your job search with each one individually and encourage them to discuss their job search with you. Reinforce the confidential nature of these conver-sations. Ask each of them if they know of one or two other current job hunters that you could include in a private and confidential job search networking group. Take it upon yourself to organize this group. Set up a regular meeting time and organize an agenda. Attend the meeting of a public group to see how it is done.

So that you have both sides of the story, I have seen a few folks who toughed out a job search almost all entirely on their own. And, yes, they all ultimately landed jobs. But it was harder, it took longer, and it was tougher on them and those around them than it had to be. Finding (or building) and using a networking support group is easier, quicker, less stressful, and more fun. What's not to like?

8. Self-Doubt, Defensiveness, and the Myth of the Perfect Job Candidate

Here is another place where my psychological training has come in handy as I guide job changers. Every human being has a weak spot. It may be in your education, your work history, your appearance, your skills, or your background. Maybe you are aware of your weak spot, maybe you aren't. Even if the world doesn't see it as a genuine weak spot, if you perceive it as such, it will work against you.

If you are in the dark about your weak spot, here's a quick way to uncover it. Complete the following sentence: *It would be a lot easier for me to get a job if only I...*

With regard to your job hunt, this is your weak spot. (This is a good exercise to do every so often during your job hunt.) When someone else raises the issue that you already believe to be a weak spot, it is only natural to want to defend yourself. But—and you've seen this in others—defensiveness negatively affects the sound of your voice, closes up your body language, stunts your creativity, makes you less open in your responses, and generally makes you a less attractive person. This is exactly what you don't want happening to you during your job search and especially during your interviews.

The way to overcome job-search defensiveness is to do a fair and honest self-assessment. You need to gain a balanced understanding of your relative strengths and weaknesses and learn how to best present them to potential employers. Perhaps you have a career counselor, out placement consultant, employment specialist, or organizational psychologist who can help you with this. You can find many helpful self-assessment exercises in one of my earlier books, *Love Your Job! Loving the Job You Have, Finding a Job You Love* (O'Reilly Media), which you can find in your library or on Amazon.com. A supportive friend or colleague can also help you with this. But whatever you do, you will need to have a clear and as objective as possible picture of who you are and what it is that you have to offer to a hiring organization. If you do not do this, you will have planted a booby-trap for yourself that will go off when you least want it to during your job search.

What is it that determines who is hired for any particular job? Is it qualifications alone? No. Is it education alone? No. Is it work experience alone? No. Is it personality alone? No. Is it references alone? No. Is it a great resume alone? No. Is it contacts alone? No. Is it luck alone? No. Is it that you bought the right book? As much as I want to say yes, the answer is no! What determines if a specific person is hired for a specific job is a) a combination of *all of these factors*, plus b) his or her ability *to communicate these factors*.

Even though you may have a great education, a strong resume, a super background, extensive work experience, and terrific personal characteristics, there may actually be someone applying for the same job as you who is *stronger* than you are in one of these categories. Does this mean that this person will certainly be hired and you will not? No. The reason is that the other candidate is probably not as strong as you are in one category or another. Every job candidate represents a unique mix of background, skills, education, knowledge, and personality, a specific equation of strengths and weaknesses.

The Myth of the Perfect Job Candidate

Unfortunately, many job hunters labor under this myth, which is based upon the unrealistic fear that applying for the same job as you is some god-like figure who is terrific in every way. It further suggests that because you are not terrific in every way, the interviewer will discover you for the imperfect, mere mortal that you are, and, thus, you will not get the job.

The way to overcome this self-doubt is to realize that there aren't very many (if any) perfect job candidates out there, and we don't live in a perfect meritocracy anyway. It is a fact that the best person for a job doesn't necessarily get hired. There will be times when this reality will work for you and there will be times when it will work against you. But that doesn't change the reality. What can help in this regard is for you to memorize Dr. Paul's #1 Rule of Successful Job Hunting: *The most effective job hunter will get the most interviews, and the most effective interviewee will get the most and the best job offers.*

Look, it's no secret to those who love you most in this world that you are nowhere close to perfect. But they still love you, right? So take a good look at your supposed weak spots; with your hard work, sense of humor, and determination to succeed, I can help you to become an effective job hunter and a terrific interviewer.

9. Your Baggage

We all drag around emotional baggage packed with unresolved, negative emotions we have collected during our lives. These emotions can come from any area of life: family, your social or personal life, your education and training, or your work life. They may have been communicated to you by parents, teachers, friends, enemies, spouses, bosses, peers, idiots, or geniuses.

Deep within each of us there is a place where we store good memories and bad, remembrances of achievements and failures, and our hopes and fears for the future. Attached to each of these are emotions. When positive emotions (love, happiness, acceptance, peacefulness, forgiveness) are touched upon by something happening in our daily lives, we are affected in both conscious and subconscious ways. Similarly, when negative emotions (fear, jealousy, dread, anger, resentment) are stirred up, we also respond in conscious and subconscious ways. Though misplaced love can have a negative effect and righteous anger can have a positive effect, we can generally say that positive emotions have a positive effect and that negative emotions have a negative effect on our daily lives. This is especially true during the job-hunting process.

If you feel that you are job searching because you were unjustly fired from your last job, the anger you feel toward your former boss may display itself in various ways during the job search. If you are envious or jealous of the position held by your interviewer, you may communicate this in your responses, your attitude, or your body language. If you are stalled by the fear of rejection or the fear of failure during your job change, you will take fewer risks and, ultimately, you may accept a job that is beneath your aspirations.

Take a good, hard look into yourself and your attitudes about job hunting. Talk them over with a close friend, confidant, mentor, or counselor. What negative emotions about this process are you carrying around? Where did they come from? What are they based on? Can you see where they might hurt you? What can you do about it? Sometimes just talking these issues through can help you to put them aside. If that is not the case, try to come up with some competing positive emotions to pair them with, to dampen their negative effect. Try to take a healthful, forgiving, and humorous look at the situations that spawned these feelings.

The negative emotions in your baggage will weigh you down, trip you up, siphon your energy, and keep you from reaching your full potential. The job hunt can be a rugged and bumpy stretch on your personal road to success. But if you dump some of that extra baggage you've been dragging along with you, you can relax a little and, I hope, even enjoy the ride.

10. The Psychology of Entitlement

A few years ago, one of my client companies asked me to do some career coaching with one of their star managers. With a BS cum laude in psychology, Marilyn had gone into consumer sales with a prestigious consumer products company right out of college. After three and a half years, she was accepted into the Wharton School of Management. After receiving her MBA, she was recruited into a widely known mutual fund company as a marketing manager. Marilyn did well with this company, but after almost five years the company was going to relocate her department to another part of the country and they wanted her to go with it.

This relocation was something that Marilyn didn't want to do, felt she didn't need to do, and when she was offered no other comparable position within the company, she informed her boss that she would rather resign than move. Her manager asked me to talk to her because a) he wanted her to change her mind and relocate, or b) if she did resign, he wanted me to explain my career coaching services, which he would offer her. She responded with something that was like a cross between disbelief and disdain.

I failed on both counts. Marilyn was dead set against relocating. Her view of the world was similar to that of the famous *New Yorker* magazine cover, with Boston and New York on the far right, a frozen, nameless tundra on the top, California on the far left, and nothing in the middle.

Her attitude about career coaching was just as parochial and short sighted—it was for losers, not high-flying winners like herself. Marilyn's attitude was that, with her educational credentials and her strong track record with great companies, she wouldn't need much help, because people would be knocking down her door looking for someone with her profile and background.

The next time I saw Marilyn was when she came up to speak to me after I had given a pro-bono speech to a local networking/support group for the unemployed—*five months* after I had last seen her! Five months isn't a particularly long job search for some jobs in some job markets, but it had seemed like a geological era to Marilyn. She had sent out a few resumes, contacted a couple of headhunters, and then she sat back to wait for the flood of wonderful offers. She was devastated that she only received a couple of courtesy phone calls in response. (I told her that with the miniscule amount of effort expended on her part, I was surprised that she had received as much response as she did.) This networking meeting was the first action step she had taken in weeks, and that was only because a close friend of hers had led her there by the hand.

The moral of this story could be about willingness to relocate or about using whatever assistance one is offered or even about humility, but it is not. The moral of this story is that no matter what type of superior background you feel that you have, no matter what credentials you've earned, no matter what prestigious educational pedigree you hold, no matter how wonderful some people have told others you are, no one is going to come knocking on your door with a basketful of wonderful and exciting career opportunities just because you feel that you are entitled to them. The psychology of entitlement—whether in your career, your family, or your community—is a roadblock to your success and satisfaction in any area of your life.

If you feel entitled to have your company, your former employer, your outplacement firm, some employment agency, a search firm, your network, or your career coach go out and find you another job, I can guarantee that you will be spending a lot of time home alone watching the soap operas and game shows.

In today's world of work, there are no guarantees and there are no entitlements. To achieve, you must push yourself to perform. To grow, you must push yourself to learn. To advance, you must strive to accept and adapt to change. The responsibility for driving and advancing your career is now, more than ever before, in your own hands. And that is as it should be.

➤➤ ➤➤ ➤➤

We've taken a hard look at the ways many people stumble during the job-hunting process. By examining the top 10 roadblocks of job hunting, I trust you now see that each of them can be overcome with knowledge, spirit, energy, humor, and optimism.

Chapter 2

Controlling Interview Anxiety

ANXIETY; ANX•I•E•TY; NOUN: A FEELING OF WORRY, NERVOUSNESS, OR UNEASE, TYPICALLY ABOUT AN IMMINENT EVENT OR SOMETHING WITH AN UNCERTAIN OUTCOME.

This is exactly what hundreds and hundreds of job candidates have reported to me before, during, and after a job interview. To a psychologist, this is 100-percent predictable because:

➤ Anxiety is a totally normal human emotion.

➤ Anxiety is experienced by every human being at some time.

➤ It is natural to be uneasy before an interview (that is, an imminent event).

➤ It is natural to be nervous during an interview (because of the relative uniqueness and rarity of the event, as well as the fact that the outcome is uncertain).

➤ It is natural to worry about the interview after it is over, not just because the outcome is uncertain but because it may negatively affect your psychological needs such as security, belonging, esteem, and self-actualization.

The anxiety response is a bequest to us from our cavemen and cave-women forebears. To survive they needed not only to respond to threats (such as a hungry tiger), but they also needed to respond to *possible* threats (such as the sound of a snapped twig which might be an approaching tiger). The ancestors of ours who responded to both actual threats and possible threats with the most epinephrine (a hormone secreted by the adrenal glands, which is why it's also called adrenaline) were most likely to live until they could, over the millennia, pass their genes down to us. You may have heard this called the "fight-or-flight response," but that is incomplete. A more accurate description is "fight, flight, or freeze" response, because it also accounts for some of our ancestors having the nerves of steel (or paralyzing fear) required to stand motionless and hopefully let the tiger pass unaware. We will address each of these responses in regard to your next interview.

Your Body on Adrenaline

Following the release of adrenaline in the body, there is increased respiration, blood circulation, and carbohydrate metabolism. These responses are designed to prepare the major muscle groups for the exertion of fighting and/or running. Increased respiration means moving more oxygen to the major muscle groups. Should this lead to hyperventilation, one may experience dizziness, lightheadedness, or even fainting. At the same time, other bodily systems such as digestion, that are nonessential for immediate survival, are being deprived of blood and oxygen, which can lead to all kinds of gastrointestinal discomfort. Another response is sweating, which is not only a cooling process but, as I have heard it opined, also causes the body to become slippery in order to make it harder for man or beast to grab you.

Have you ever noticed how during a scary scene in a movie, the hairs on your arms or the back of your neck stand up and your fingers or toes tingle? These, too, are adrenaline responses. As muscles tense from adrenaline, your chest may feel constricted or painful. Often, adrenaline will cause the pupils in your eyes to dilate to let in more light, which can distort what you're looking at with unnatural brightness or give it an appearance of unreality.

I will say this again and again: these reactions are totally human, totally normal, and totally predictable. Maybe you'll only experience one or two of these reactions. Sometimes you may not experience any of them. Sometimes, in very stressful situations, you may experience more than a few. But at some time or other you *will* experience them. And this is not all bad!

Managing Your Interview Anxiety

Interview anxiety can be managed. By learning to do so, you will be directing all that survival energy not just into surviving the interview but also into improving your overall interview performance. You will be able to think and respond more quickly. You will be able to recall your career-related stories in better detail. You will appear more relaxed, yet alert and engaging. You will have more control over the tone and pitch of your voice. You will be more physically comfortable. You will be better able to address any mistakes. Should you encounter one of those rare stress interviews, you will not get rattled, but rather be able to deal with it constructively. You will know what to expect. You will be able to gauge your performance and continue to improve your interviewing skills.

For years I have asked successful interviewers how they have managed to control their interview anxiety. If I heard of any technique, idea, or method being helpful more than a half dozen times, it made it into my research file. For the first time ever I am publicly releasing this list that I have used with my private career coaching clients to help them control, manage, and overcome their interview anxiety. Not every technique will work for every job hunter. And they are not magic solutions; you've got to put them to work. But if interviewing anxiety has ever been an issue for you, I am confident there is something here that can help you achieve a new level of interviewing success.

Here's How: Before the Interview

Your goal is not to eliminate anxiety. Your goal is to channel that energy which will control it. Every interviewer expects job candidates to be a little nervous.

Recognize it for what it is: a two-way conversation, not an interrogation. They are assessing you and you are assessing them.

Keep it in perspective. You may get a job offer. You may not get a job offer. These are the only two possible results, and one of them is really good news. Nobody gets frog-walked to the parking lot, nobody gets sent to Siberia, and nobody gets shot. The worst that can happen is that you'll come out the way you went in.

Prepare what you'll say. In Chapter 10, you will find Tool #7 devoted to the most frequently asked interview questions. Go through that list and select the ones that you're most concerned about. Write down in shorthand some strong answers and then practice them aloud until the anxiety recedes. Don't try to memorize. Just use the questions as prompts for the thoughts you want to use to help sell yourself.

Prepare what you'll ask. Usually you will have the opportunity to ask a few questions toward the end of the interview. From your research (you did research the employer, right?), ask a couple of questions that demonstrate your preliminary knowledge of the organization and which wisely identify a couple of issues important to your potential role.

Research the interviewer. The interviewer already knows a good deal about you before you meet her. It only makes sense for you to use any Web, industry, company, or personal resources to get a sense of the person who will be interviewing you. You might find a tidbit that will help you discover a common interest or experience.

Practice, practice, practice. In Chapter 5, you will find instructions regarding a professional approach to practice your interviewing skills. This is the single most powerful way to improve your interviewing skills. In Chapter 10, you will find practice interview tools #9 and #10 that have helped thousands of job hunters move their interview skills from good to great. Practicing your skills is the surest way for you to control your interview anxiety and outperform your competition.

Do a test run to confirm that you know the best route to the interview and how long it will take to get there at that time of day. Do not depend on your GPS, MapQuest, Google Maps, or any such service.

Select your outfit or a couple of favorite outfits. Choose clothes in which you look good and feel comfortable, that are clean, neat, fit well, and are not brand new. Keep them aside exclusively for interviewing and you'll always be ready for a last-minute interview. Remember the general rule of dressing for one step up the ladder from the job you want. And I'll say this repeatedly: no flip-flops—*ever.*

Schedule only one per day. Between the stress beforehand and the letdown afterward, you will be tired. Unless you are an expert at the process, it is unlikely you will be at your best twice in a day.

Pack your stuff. By this I mean the stuff you'll be bringing with you to the interview. This includes directions to get you there ahead of time, several copies of your resume, your reference information, a couple of pens, a notebook, business cards, your calendar, cell phone, and a minimal amount of personal care items (for example, mints, and a comb, not an entire cosmetics counter or drugstore). Collect all this stuff the night before in the briefcase or attaché case that you'll be carrying.

Get a good night's sleep or at least a full night's rest. This is not a good time to experiment with sleeping aids, as many can leave you groggy in the morning.

Here's How: The Morning of the Interview

Get up early. Don't risk an alarm clock malfunction. Give yourself adequate wake-up time. Rushing around is counterproductive to being relaxed.

Cut back on the caffeine. Remember, the attitude you're looking to project is relaxed, alert, and cool, not edgy and jagged. Eat something; your body needs energy, and a growling stomach isn't a great selling point.

Relax. What helps you relax? Meditation works for some folks. Visualization works for others. Deep breathing or yoga work for still others. Some great interviewers give themselves positive affirmations; others exercise (but not too strenuously). Some folks read; others listen to a favorite comedy routine. But whatever works for you, don't overdo it. Remember, we're going for relaxed, alert, and cool, not totally spaced out and eerie.

Use music to help tune you up emotionally. There is great power in music. If you need to relax more, there is plenty of music to help you do that. If you need to ramp up your energy level, there are many pieces from rock to classical to really get your blood flowing. Prepare a playlist to use in either situation.

Get there a bit early. Ten to 15 minutes will do. This gives you enough time to hit the restroom, check the mirror, and try out that winning smile. If you have an emergency, use the cell phone you packed last night. But because you already tried out the route and traffic, neither of those should be an emergency.

Dry your hands. Nobody likes a wet, clammy handshake. Take special care if you just washed them. If you get sweaty palms due to stress, use your handkerchief; do not put them in your pockets or hang them, clenched, down at your side. Position them on your lap, with palms up and fingers spread, so the air will help them stay dry. Straighten your back, take a few deep breaths, and think a positive thought.

Here's How: During the Interview

Breathe and smile. Most of the time these things come naturally, but they may not if you are anxious or really concentrating.

Listen. Let the interviewer complete his or her question or thought before jumping in with a response. Focusing your attention on the other person is a good way to lower your anxiety about how you are doing. You may want to take an occasional note.

Think. If a question seems to come from left field or is one you haven't given much thought, feel free to take a minute to frame your response. You may even want to say something like, "Wow, good question, let me think." You're a human being, not a gumball machine that immediately pops out an answer when a question is asked. Thinking is not only allowed, it's encouraged.

Get in your questions. You prepared them and they're good ones. When it feels like the clock is starting to run down, try saying something along the lines of "I have a couple of questions that I'm hoping you might be able to address." Most interviewers will welcome them. Here is a good place to check your notes. Listen carefully to your interviewer's responses and take notes as appropriate. If the interview has had a real give-and-take feel to it, you may have been able to get your questions in earlier.

Use your "close." You always want to close your interview on the strongest possible note. See Chapter 7 for detailed instructions on how to accomplish this.

Remember your manners. Thank the interviewer for his/her time. Do so even if it felt like it was a terrible interview; for all you know, the interviewer may have thought it went well.

Follow up. Ask where the employer is in the hiring process and when they hope to make a decision. Ask when it would be appropriate for you to touch base and "see where they are in the process." Determine if e-mail or a telephone call is preferred.

Here's How: After the Interview

Complete the post-interview tool in Chapter 10 while the experience is freshest in your mind. This tool will help you evaluate and improve your interview performance.

Follow through. If you promised to send your interviewer any additional information, certifications, licenses, and so on, be sure to do so as soon as possible.

A personal thank-you note is mandatory. It demonstrates your courtesy and is a great opportunity to continue to express your interest in the assignment.

Congratulate yourself. You did it! You're now one interview closer to the job you want. Meet a friend for coffee, see a movie, go for a swim, play with your dog, whatever—but do something fun to reward yourself.

Begin anew. Now is the time to start preparing for your next interview. And your next interview will be better than your last one. You will be better prepared, have more experience under your belt, have identified places where you can improve your skills, and be less anxious.

Controlling Interview Anxiety Is an Ongoing Process

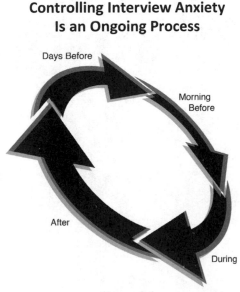

Figure 2.1

➤➤ ➤➤ ➤➤

In closing this chapter, I'd like to draw your attention to Figure 2.1 on the previous page. Its purpose is to reinforce my message that controlling your interview anxiety is a constant, ongoing process. Interview stress, performance anxiety, or plain old bothersome nervousness can surface at any time. You now know that this is perfectly natural. The only surefire method to control it is to use as many of the 30 methods I've described in this chapter to address it—head on—at every stage of the interview process.

Chapter 3

Where Are All the Damn Jobs?

In Chapter 1, you learned Dr. Paul's #1 Rule of Successful Job Hunting: *The most effective job hunter will get the most interviews, and the most effective interviewee will get the most and the best job offers.* In Chapter 2, you learned how to identify, control, and manage the very natural anxiety that every interviewer experiences. In Chapter 3, you are going to learn how to land more interviews for better jobs.

Many job hunters want to jump right into the interviewing process without realizing that there is a process that can be mastered if one wants to uncover more opportunities, uncover them sooner, and avoid wasting a lot of valuable time wandering around lost for some undetermined amount of time, asking anyone who will listen, "Hey, where are all the jobs?" Before you can be a great interviewer, you must become an effective job hunter.

An effective job hunter is someone who is out there in the marketplace actively looking for new opportunities—with knowledge, with energy, and with focus. When I'm at a social gathering and people hear what I do for a living and what I write about, I often get comments such as, "I'd like a better job," or, "I'm keeping my eyes open," or, "I'll take a look if something interesting comes along." With my wife's help, I've learned to button my yap, smile, and nod supportively (while looking for a beverage refill). Prior to the civilizing effect that Linda has had on me, I used to get on my high horse and try to motivate these folks with the facts of job-hunting life. These people aren't job hunters; they're more like relaxed weekend bird-watchers. Maybe something will come along, maybe it won't. They are passively waiting and hoping for a more satisfying career. Don't get me wrong: patience and hope are great virtues, but winning in the job-hunting game takes drive, savvy, and a willingness to take risks.

Realistic, Market-Tuned Goal-Setting

If you were planning a vacation or a major trip, how would you go about it? Most likely you would do a number of things before you ever made reservations to spend your hard-earned money. You would research the area you wanted to visit. You would make a list of the things you most enjoy doing, and then you'd find out if your destination offers them. You would find out what all this costs. You would take inventory of what you have and make a list of what you need. You would ask family, friends, neighbors, and contacts for their ideas and input. In short, you would put together an informed plan of how to accomplish what you want to do on your vacation.

Embarking on an effective job hunt requires exactly this kind of thinking and planning. Before you ever step out into the job market, I want you to know the lay of the land. Certainly, you will learn a lot more than what immediately meets the eye as your job hunt progresses, but, even just starting out, I want you to know more than your competition. To get your job hunt up and running as quickly and efficiently as possible, you need to know the answers to the following questions right off the bat:

1. Who are the potential employers in my target geographical area?
2. Of these employers, which ones employ people with my skills, in my functional area?
3. Where can I learn about their history, products, and services?
4. Where do these employers advertise for help?

5. What employment agencies and executive recruiters do they use?

6. What online job listing or Web recruiting services do they use?

7. What is the typical pay or salary range for people with my skills in these types of organizations?

Perhaps you are a skilled and creative researcher and already have some ideas about where to find this essential job-hunting information. Perhaps a few taps on your keyboard deliver instant access to everything you need to know. If so, great. But for most of us, just the word *research* brings back memories of all the dull school projects we once struggled with. Regardless of how skilled you are as a researcher or how you feel about tracking down hard-to-find information, I have great news for you! You have, at your disposal, a knowledgeable and willing partner who will advise and consult with you in the research process. Oh, and I forgot to mention—this help won't cost you a penny.

Your New Best Friend

Your new best friend works downtown or maybe downtown in the next town over or maybe at the local college. He or she is a reference librarian. By nature, these people like to know where information can be found, and, by professional training, they know how to find it. If you haven't visited the reference department of your local library lately, it's time to get your butt in there.

What you will find are hundreds and sometimes thousands of resources you can use in your job hunt: books about job hunting and interviewing, directories of employers, research guides to various industries, annual reports of companies you might want to work for, access to online databases for research, and Websites with job listings. It is a veritable treasure trove of valuable job-hunting information. Most libraries are members of library networks, and if you can't find something in your own library, the reference librarian can help you find material from all over the country.

But (you knew there had to be a *but*, didn't you?) your reference librarian is not your personal researcher. She is not there to wait on you hand and foot. You are not the only person who needs research help. She is there to teach you, to advise you, and to consult with you about how you can find the information you need. Be satisfied with this valuable and unexpected source of help, and learn how to dig out the information that will help you land a job you love.

When you first decide you are going to go job hunting, review the seven questions listed previously. With whatever resources you have already at hand, list all the relevant information you can. Then, when you have already begun the research process, go introduce yourself to the reference department at your local library. If your local library is not too great, try one in a neighboring town or at a local college. It's important to have started the process before you even go to the library for two reasons:

1. I want you to see how difficult it can be to find out what you need to know.

2. I want you to show your reference librarian that you have started on your own, that you know what you're looking for, that you realize her professional assistance is of great value to you, and that you are a willing student and will not be a drain on her time and patience. Alienating your local reference librarian is one of the worst things you can do when you're job hunting (or writing a book, or just trying to live an informed life).

When you first introduce yourself to the reference librarian, start by asking what resources are on hand that other job hunters have found most useful. I know the job hunt can be an isolating process, but you are not out there alone, nor are you the first person who has stumbled into the library looking for help. The librarian will ask you what type of job you are looking for and what types of organizations you're looking to find out about. This is another reason why it is essential for you to have thought this stuff through before you go in looking for help. The more informed you get on your own, the more help the librarian can be. Librarians like people who are willing to work at it. But remember our *but*: they are not there to do the research for you; they are there to guide you, advise you, and help you do it on your own. Be appreciative and thankful.

With this research process well underway, you now should have enough preliminary information to identify your initial job-hunting goals. You are already miles ahead of your competition, most of whom are working from inaccurate assumptions about the job market, rumors about who is hiring, faulty or out-of-date job-hunting techniques, or just plain wondering where the damn jobs are. Your goals are realistic and market-tuned because they are based on current, accurate, and objective data. Congratulations, you're off to a great start.

How to Effectively Identify Your Job Targets

You now have your preliminary goals firmly in mind: you are looking for this type of job in this type of organization. Such organizations typically recruit and hire people through these avenues; and they typically pay people with your skills about this much money. What you need now are specific job targets.

There are dozens of different ways you can identify bona fide job targets, but, generally speaking, they all fit into one of four major job-hunting methods. These four methods, which I call the *four-front job campaign*, are: published openings, cold-contacting, recruiters, and networking. (Of course, there's always marrying for money or winning the lottery, but those are topics for other books.)

Published Openings

Help-Wanted Ads

Most people are familiar with this tried and true job-hunting method: the help-wanted ads. Some appear in your local paper, some in the local business press, and others in the major metropolitan papers. There are fewer of them (both newspapers and help-wanted ads) every month, but you shouldn't overlook them.

Published openings appear in other places than just the newspaper. Some are in technical journals, professional newsletters, union job banks, and state unemployment office listings. We'll address the issue of online job boards shortly.

Job Fairs

Job fairs are good opportunities to locate published openings in organizations that are hiring. If you can make a personal contact, ask for a business card, see if there are any appropriate openings, leave a resume, and follow up later. But if a table or booth is mobbed, I suggest that you do not just throw your resume onto a pile, hoping it will come to someone's notice later on. Try to get a business card from whoever is representing the company (usually a rep from human resources). You can follow up personally by e-mail or phone later, stating that you were in attendance and unable to get through the crush of people, but would like to uncover any openings that might be a fit for your background.

Job Boards

You've been to the big job boards everyone knows, such as Monster.com and CareerBuilder.com. If you're lucky, you find something that looks good, you hit the submit button, and then you wait. The good news is that you feel like you've actually done something productive. It's fast, it's easy, it's encouraging ("Hey, look at all the jobs out there"), and you're protected from the disappointment of personal rejection. If you have some specific quality, skill, or experience that makes you stand out from the thousands of other folks who just did what you did, you may receive an e-mail back in response. But using job boards (or any job-hunting method) exclusively is a recipe for disaster.

The numbers are against you. The *Wall Street Journal* reported that large firms can get 400 board responses a day. Two studies I've seen recently put the percentage of new hires from job boards at 10–12 percent (with a strong suggestion that those numbers might be too high). More to the point is that relying on job boards ignores a central truth of job hunting: no one hires a resume. Getting hired requires some kind of personal connection.

Does this mean you should ignore job boards? No. What it *does* mean is that you should use them wisely and allocate time and energy to them in proportion to the positive results they give you.

Aggregators

One way to cut through the clutter is to use a job board aggregator such as Simplyhired.com or Careerjet.com. New ones come and old ones go at a fast clip, so do your own current research. Just recently, a client landed a very good job he first identified via Indeed.com (and I promised him I'd mention it even though I'd not heard of it before). Aggregators collect, sort, and display postings from multiple job boards, sort of like one-stop shopping. Plug in your job and geographic preferences and you're off to the races. Some boards have ads for jobs that don't exist, for jobs that have been filled, or ads for alleged career consultants that are often one jump ahead of a process server or the better business bureau.

Aggregators have a good reputation for sorting the wheat from the chaff, but as always, use your alert consumer skills.

Niche Boards

Just as it sounds, a niche job board limits its job listings to those in specific functions or industries, certain geographic targets, or other interests. They are a worthwhile place to look for openings that may not be posted by the larger boards or aggregators. Thus, you may be competing with a smaller batch of competitors for any one position. There are too many to suggest favorites, and you should search on your own for those that most closely meet your needs. But to give you an idea of what to look for, here are some that have a good reputation:

- **Accounting:** Accountingjobstoday.com.
- **Jobs in Australia:** Seek.com.au.
- **The Arts:** Artjob.org.
- **Biotech/Pharmaceuticals:** Medzilla.com.
- **Jobs in Canada:** Workopolis.com.
- **Communications/Public Relations:** Prsa.org/jobcenter.
- **Construction:** Constructionjobs.com.
- **Diversity Recruiting:** Hirediversity.com.
- **Engineering:** Engineerjobs.com.
- **Electrical Engineers:** EEE.org.
- **Finance:** Fins.com/finance.
- **Government:** Usajobs.gov.
- **Healthcare:** Healthjobsusa.com.
- **Higher Education:** Higheredjobs.com.
- **Human Resources:** Jobs.shrm.org.
- **Marketing:** Talentzoo.com.
- **Nonprofits:** Idealist.org.
- **Older workers:** Eons.com and Grayhairmanagement.com.
- **Science:** Naturejobs.com.
- **Sports:** Workinsports.com.
- **Technology:** Dice.com.

The online employment world is huge and can be a major time vacuum. Do not cruise the Web looking for appropriate sites during the valuable 9-to-5 hours when it is most convenient to make personal contact with folks. If you are currently employed, this goes double for you, because it is hugely unwise (as well as unethical) to use your employer's computer or time to pursue these avenues.

The good news is that regardless of where these published openings are found, 99.9 percent of them represent real jobs at real organizations that are looking to hire. The bad news is that any informed and motivated job hunter has access to the same job leads you do. As a result, this lowers your odds of landing a job via this method. Some surveys say that published openings of all kinds account for only 5 percent of the jobs filled annually in the United States. Other estimates are as high as 12 to 15 percent. But whatever tomorrow's statistics on this method are, it accounts for thousands and thousands of jobs. And just how many jobs are you looking for?

Cold-Contacting

This is another traditional job-hunting method. From your library and online research, you identify a number of employers in your geographical target area that you think might need your skills. Using your research skills, you identify the name of an appropriate line manager or human resources person to whom you send a cover letter and resume either by mail or e-mail. You do this a few places at a time, which allows you time to follow up on each submission personally. Within a given period of time (which you stated in your letter), you follow up with a phone call to make sure your resume was received and to see if any appropriate openings exist. It's as easy as that.

This method has somewhat fallen into disfavor because some people misuse it so badly. They take a huge, generic list, do a mass mailing "to whom it may concern," and then sit back and wait for something to happen. And usually nothing does. The only person to whom your job hunt may concern is you. Don't expect some unknown, faceless stranger to lurch out of nowhere and hire you. It just ain't gonna happen.

Used properly, cold-contacting can be a very effective way of uncovering leads in what has been referred to as the "hidden job market." A certain number of times a resume just happens to cross someone's desk at the time a job opens up or is about to open up. Some estimate that this approach may account for about 5 to 10 percent of all jobs filled annually.

Some employers prefer job candidates to e-mail resumes directly to them at the company's own Website. This is a great method because many organizations have software that can cross-reference your skills with openings they may have anywhere in the world. But don't abandon traditional ideas while trying out new ones; having a personal contact or endorsement will help get that e-mailed resume to the right person's desk.

Recruiters

There is an entire employee recruiting industry devoted to helping organizations hire the right person for the right job. This industry, which some studies say accounts for 15 to 20 percent of yearly hires, is made up of temporary employment agencies, contracting agencies, contingency employment agencies, and retained executive search firms. Some of these companies will say they do all of the above, but common sense should tell you that this makes about as much sense as having your dentist offer to do your colonoscopy. The best recruiters have specialties and are experts in one aspect of the employment industry. The employment professionals with whom you want to be working are those who work with people at your level, in your function, and in your industry.

Temp agencies (just as they sound) help organizations line up temporary help. Sometimes these temp assignments turn into full-time jobs; most of the time they do not. In this category are the firms that hire for contract jobs in different locations. They are often called travel firms.

Contract agencies are similar to temp agencies, although the time frame and scope of the assignment are usually spelled out in greater detail.

Contingency employment agencies (many also call themselves executive recruiters) generally help companies hire people at salary levels between $20,000 and $90,000. They get paid only if a job candidate they refer to an employer is hired; thus, their fee is "contingent." Some are not very selective as to who they refer for interviews, whereas many others are quite professional. You'll need to assess this on a firm-to-firm basis.

Retained executive search firms generally place executives at the $70,000 level and above. They are paid "on retainer" whether or not they fill the position. Naturally, those firms that keep fees but don't end up completing their assignments don't stay around very long. The best search firms are exceptionally selective because they guarantee to redo the search (a several-month-long process) if the selected candidate doesn't work out.

How to Work With a Recruiter

The way you get recruiters to help you during your job hunt is quite straightforward. Identify the recruiters who are specialists in your industry, who work in your functional area, and who work in your part of the world. The best recruiter to work with is one with whom you've already developed a relationship. The second best recruiter to work with is one to whom you've been personally referred. Should neither of those approaches work for you, identify appropriate recruiters online or via your public library reference section. Some resources are free (such as Rileyguide.com or Searchfirm.com), and others are not (such as the classic, red-covered *Directory of Executive and Professional Recruiters*). This is a good place to remind you that many of your job-hunting related expenses are deductible under certain circumstances on your Federal income tax return. For more on this go to Chapter 10 and review Tool #3: Tax Tips for the Job Hunter.

Use what information you gather and follow each recruiter's instructions as to making contact. Typically, you will send them a cover letter and resume alerting them to your availability. That's it. The end, *finito, hasta la vista,* baby. Don't call them; don't pester them with e-mails; don't drop in unannounced and offer to take them to coffee, lunch, drinks, or Disney World.

The best way to get your resume shredded by a headhunter is to be a pain in the butt. Why? Because recruiters *don't* find jobs for people. Recruiters find people for jobs. (Repeat these last two sentences until you understand them.) If you have the skills or background for an assignment that a headhunter is working on, she will be in touch with you. That's what headhunters do; that's how they make their living. If you have a particularly unique or interesting background, you may receive a courtesy call to let you know that you're now in their database for future searches. But what they don't do is spend the day chatting with job hunters or giving career advice or trying to find you a job. It's not that they don't like you or don't value your background; it's that they are not in the advice business.

Some good news here is that no reputable employment agency or recruiter will ever charge you a fee. The hiring organization is the recruiter's client, and they pay the fee. Remember, job hunting can be so hard that you can't even pay someone to do it for you. You may find that there are some crooks out there that will take your money and promise to find you a job—but they won't. Save your money. If you have an uncontrollable urge to throw your money away, feel free to send it to me. Of course, I won't find you a job either, but at least I won't lie to you about it!

Networking

So much has been written about networking that some tree-hugger types actually break out into tears whenever the term is used. Networking is made out to be a lot more complicated than it really is. A quick definition may help. Networking: *the ongoing process of asking people* (some of whom you know and some of whom you'll meet along the way) to give you information that will be helpful to your job hunt. That's it.

Obviously, the big kahuna, the key piece of information you really want to find, is the name of the place where there is a great job ready and waiting for you. But the reality is that most people don't have that information for you. And if that's the only question you ask ("I'm looking for a job. Do you have any leads for me?"), then you will have pretty much wasted your network contacts. This is the biggest networking mistake job hunters make, and it can add months to a job search. They list their contacts, and then go through the list checking off names as they call, asking for job leads. Then they sit back and say, "See, networking doesn't work."

Your contacts have tons of really helpful information for you, but you have to know what it is and how to specifically ask for it. Most people are willing to help you, but you have to help them help you. You can ask for:

➻   Names of places to look for published openings.

➻   Names of job boards and Websites that other job hunters have found useful.

➻   Great libraries or names of reference librarians who are especially knowledgeable or helpful.

➻   Local college, university, or alumni job-hunting resources.

➻ Names of recruiters working in your state, industry, or functional area.

➻ Locations of local job-hunting support groups.

➻ Names of growing/hiring local companies.

➻ How your resume looks; how your phone voice sounds.

➻ And, *most importantly,* who in their contact network might be helpful to you in your job hunt.

This last item is especially important because you must be expanding your contact network continuously during the job hunt. You must never run out of people to contact; this is the biggest key to networking success. Start by listing every contact you can think of. (Use Tool #6: Building Your Contact Network, from the Toolkit in Chapter 10.) Then, as you work your way through your contacts, train yourself to ask for the names of four or five people whom your contacts think may have some job hunting-related information that could be helpful to you. This is essential to expanding your network.

Some of your contacts may resist, whereas some may be very helpful right off the bat. You may have to spend some time educating others about how the networking process works. You may need to call some back a second or third time to give them time to dig up some helpful information for you.

In my decades of helping people change jobs and build careers, I have observed a somewhat counterintuitive phenomenon. I call it the "strength of weak ties." Most of your initial contacts will give you a lead or two, a piece of information, and maybe the names of one or two people to contact. This is a fine way to start. But I have observed that the further you build your network *away* from your first-level contacts, the *more* helpful people are: the more leads they share, the more ideas they generate, the more contact names they give you. I have a couple of theories about why this is true, but that's not important here. What is crucial to your job hunt is that you force yourself to build your network beyond your own personal contacts. That's where you will find the power of networking, and that is why study after study indicates that about 70 percent of the jobs filled annually are filled as a result of a contact made through networking.

Maximizing Today's Technology

The four basic job-hunting methods haven't changed in a hundred years. But thanks to rapid technological advances, there are some new tools that can make the job search more productive—*if* you know how to use them. As with any new tool or approach, there are some things to be wary of, and I'll mention them as well.

E-mailing Resumes, Letters, and References

For starters I suggest setting up a separate e-mail account that you use only for job hunting. This is for privacy and security. It is far too easy to miss an important job-search e-mail if it goes to your at-home, family, or (gulp) former or present employer's e-mail address. Also, this gives you a chance to come up with a professional sounding address and get rid of surferboi411 or goth-chick89. Never use your a work e-mail address, because it does not belong to you; it belongs to your employer. If employed, remember to find and use the blocking feature that many Websites have so your employer doesn't learn that you are out there looking.

We are all familiar with the speed with which documents can be transmitted via the Internet. Anything that speeds up the job hunt is a blessing. For starters, identify yourself on the e-mail subject line. Make sure you have accurately labeled any documents you are attaching. I suggest a labeling format with your last name, first name, and what it is (for example, resume, cover letter, references). Universal communication between systems has improved but is not yet perfect, so you need to be sure whatever you are sending can be downloaded and read on the other end. You certainly don't want your resume to end up looking like hieroglyphics. One way to do this is to only attach documents that are in easily transferable typefaces such as Times New Roman and Arial. Microsoft Word is your safest bet.

A better and safer way to achieve this is to convert the document you're attaching to a PDF (Portable Document Format). This file format essentially takes a picture of your document that is easily transmittable, maintains its integrity, and can't be easily changed or edited by anyone else. Your Print menu page has this option on it (or ask any fourth grader how to do it). E-mail attachments can often contain computer viruses, so one way to reassure potential employers is to make your e-mail note your cover letter and attach your specifically named resume to reduce or remove the perception of risk on the receiving end. Even if your e-mailed application or resume does not bounce back to you, I suggest that you make a quick phone call to ensure that your materials have been received.

Cell Phones, Smart Phones, and PDAs

These tools can keep you connected with the outside world 24/7. This is a double-edged sword for all of us, and the job hunter is no exception. The obvious downside is the potential loss of privacy and having work (or your job search) intrude into your personal or family time. The benefits to the job hunter far outweigh any negatives because these tools can greatly facilitate making contacts, scheduling meetings, arranging interviews, and following up.

DO:

➤➤ Set up your voice/text/e-mail. Check it/them for accuracy.

➤➤ Leave a friend a voice mail. Listen to your voice and make any adjustment needed to sound as professional as possible.

➤➤ Keep voice mails and text messages brief and businesslike.

➤➤ Use someone else's phone to verify that your outgoing message is clearly audible and professional sounding.

➤➤ Recharge your device nightly.

➤➤ Check your phone/PDA voice mail and phone and text logs regularly.

➤➤ Make it a habit to turn off these devices prior to every meeting/interview.

DON'T:

➤➤ Answer or return a call or pick up messages from a moving vehicle or a noisy location.

➤➤ Engage in any conversation where you may be overheard.

➤➤ Pick up or respond to messages while waiting for a meeting or interview; use that time to focus on your strategy and goals for the meeting.

➤➤ Answer any call or respond to any message until you are sure who it is from and you are prepared to respond positively and professionally.

Social Media/Social Networking

Effective job hunting and landing great interviews require that you communicate with as much of the world as possible. Intelligent and savvy use of electronic media and social networks can have a significant effect on one's career progress. Those who are trying to make gobs of money from these tools only hype the positive effects—and, yes, they are many. However, as your "coach between the covers" (as one reader so saucily referred to me), it's up to me to point out both the obvious and not-so-obvious mistakes you can make.

On one hand, you need to understand that any positive effect, such as raising your profile and acquainting others with who you are and what you have to offer, may not be immediate and is apt to be long term. On the other hand, you should also realize that a negative effect can be almost instantaneous if you risk damaging your image by presenting yourself in anything less than a mature, professional manner. If you are a novice with these tools and methods, start off slowly, cautiously, and conservatively. If you are an experienced user, don't forget that they are like power tools: incredibly effective and yet incredibly destructive (especially when used with adult beverages).

Currently, there are dozens of social networking sites, boasting users in the tens of millions. Some so-called experts declare that social networking will replace traditional job-hunting techniques because of its phenomenal growth and ubiquity. This is a completely erroneous notion. These social networking sites are not job-hunting *techniques*; they are job-hunting *tools*. And in the same way a hammer cannot build anything without it being used skillfully, a social networking site cannot land you a great interview without being skillfully used.

That said, social networking sites are valuable tools that can be used to more effectively and more rapidly pursue each of the four traditional job-search methods. You can use your online contacts to:

➻ Identify published openings.

➻ Cold contact hiring managers or potential employers.

➻ Find helpful inside information about target employers and interviewers.

➻ Locate recruiters who work in your industry or function.

➻ Refresh and expand your existing network exponentially.

The wide-open forum that is the Web contains more material on social networking and job hunting than can be summarized here. Further, it is hard to identify genuine user feedback. Some positive reports are little more than corporate viral marketing efforts. Some negative reports are merely the venting of disappointed job hunters who have learned that effective social networking actually requires knowledge, time, and energy.

In the last 24 months I have compiled feedback from 844 job hunters in six countries (United States, Canada, UK, Ireland, Germany, and France) who are actively using or have used social media to help them land a new job. The following results of my research do not represent the final word on this topic, but rather present a current snapshot of job hunters' experiences using social media to help them find employment.

- After finding a job opening via *any* method, it has become a common strategy to search your social network(s) for those who might give you valuable insight into the organizational structure and culture, as well as anyone who might actually help you get in the door. This includes former employees, current employees, association executives, vendors, or suppliers.
- More than ever before, human resources professionals and executive recruiters frequently Google job candidates and check social sites to see what background information is available about them. If they recognize a contact held in common, it is not unusual for them to check out the candidate before ever speaking with him or her.
- Most job hunters indicate that it is more productive to start with a list of target employers and then search for contacts (such as current or former employees) than it is to search for posted job openings.
- Job candidates frequently report how frustrating it is when contacting someone they don't actually know. What helps is to do your homework first, see if you have a contact in common, and then have that person introduce you. Otherwise, learn what you can about them and their organization, and tailor your approach using any commonality, or "hook," that you can.

With these general observations in mind, let's look at some of the most popular sites.

LinkedIn.com

LinkedIn is both the largest business/professional networking site (300 million members as of this writing) and the network most preferred by employers. Your free account makes it easy for you to post your background and recommendations; link with colleagues, former coworkers, friends from school, and influencers; and join interest groups. If you are job hunting "in the open," I suggest posting that you are "seeking a new opportunity" or "job hunting." Check out and consider joining the Job-Hunt Help LinkedIn group.

Plaxo.com

Plaxo is another business-focused site. Its easy interface is great for managing your contacts and keeping track of them as they progress in their careers. With a current e-mail address, Plaxo will request an update whenever someone's situation changes. No more lost references, no more lost contacts.

Zoominfo.com

Some sophisticated job hunters have shared with me that they use this site in their job hunting even though it is not a social networking site per se. In fact, it is primarily a business-to-business search engine that can help you research contacts at your target organizations. You'll need to claim your own profile, post a photo, and even correct any errors on your profile so that any employer who is researching you can get an accurate handle on your background. There are a couple of levels: one is free, and the other has a fee and provides detailed information.

Yahoogroups.com and Google Plus (https//plus.google.com)

You may want to consider visiting one of these sites if you have enough time to participate in e-mail discussion groups, or join "Circles" (private, user-defined contact groups) and "Hangouts" (user-created video chats), or find a locally focused, networking, job-hunting advice and moral support group. I may be underselling the value of these sites, especially in areas that are quite rural (as suggested to me by one fervent job-hunting user of both). I welcome your input on this for future editions of this book. That said, not many job hunters have said that these sites are worth the investment of time they have spent on them. And a very few job hunters have admitted that they use these sites and others like them to avoid getting out there and actually interacting with real people.

Facebook.com

Facebook is the largest social network. On one hand, if you have hundreds of "friends," you should be informing them of your job hunt and suggest ways they can help you, such as referring you to helpful recruiters, connecting with friends of theirs in any of your target employers, and, in general, informing them of what it is that you're looking for. If, however, you are job hunting while employed, I would direct you to any of the numerous articles on the problems Facebook has had regarding users' privacy. I advise that you go to Account, then Privacy Settings; choose "Friends Only." Your Facebook profile should be private, so learn about the privacy settings and choose accordingly. There is no reason for a potential employer to be perusing your personal updates, but many employers can't help themselves if you leave this door open.

Twitter.com

Twitter is a microblogging service that allows users to post and send messages of up to 140 characters known as tweets. These tweets can be displayed on the author's profile and sent to the author's "followers." Twitter's statistics are mind-blowing. With 135,000 new Twitter users signing up *every day*, there are now 645,750,000 registered users. Trying to get a message out? Consider that there are 190 million unique Twitter visitors every month. The only explanation I can come up with for this explosive growth is that 140 characters are quite sufficient for one thought in an era of ever-shorter attention spans, and constant media bombardment, and when bumper-sticker idioms are the essence of political and social debate.

Much of what you find on Twitter supports the often-dismissive comments about it being a frivolous waste of time. Many celebrities and politicians hire staff to pump out inconsequential tweets on an hourly basis to foster the illusion that you actually have some kind of relationship with them. For them it's just another form of advertising. Frankly, I don't care where my favorite musician or actor buys his socks or what he had for lunch. And if such gibberish isn't fodder for the stalkers out there, then I don't know what is.

If you know who you want to follow on Twitter or if you what organization you want to gather real-time information about, or want to try to make a connection inside of a company where you currently have no contacts from your existing social network, then Twitter may be your new best friend. Again, as with all these technological tools and services, I urge you to explore and use Twitter only in the hours when personal or face-to-face contact is difficult or impossible. Only after becoming conversant with its usage do I suggest that you include it in your daily job-hunting regimen.

As with most networking—social or otherwise—the best time to develop your network (or Twitter followers) is when you don't need them and when you're out there building your reputation. You can do this by following the industry you're interested in and the thought leaders in your field, as well as engaging with people who are a rung or two above you in your chosen field with whom you might not otherwise interact.

Another great reason to use Twitter is to offer help to those who are looking for networking help themselves. When others are looking for ideas and contacts, be as generous as you can, because this will often come back to benefit you. It establishes you not only for what you know, but for what kind of a human being you are. Using Twitter solely for self-promotion is a huge turnoff. Share information, share resources, and share shortcuts. Realize that what you share will be reviewed not only for what it says, but also for what it says about you.

Lastly, many organizations have Twitter handles. Finding and following them can help you get an inside track on job openings of interest before they are officially posted to the world. Twitter has a certain informality about it that can be both good and bad. Use it to showcase your wit and personality, but don't let it beguile you into thinking that you are just chatting with your pals. Professional, polite, and supportive beats snide and dismissive every time.

Blogging

A blog (a mashup of *Web Log*) is a Web-based journal in which you can establish yourself as an expert, commentator, or observer of the issues and topics in which you are most interested. It is not like just posting an article somewhere, because one of the most popular aspects of blogs is interactivity. That is, readers can comment on your post or respond to others who have responded. It is a good way to promote your business or profession or share your thoughts on a subject that you love. You can raise your profile in a specific area by launching your own blog or by becoming a regular commentator on someone else's. Setting up and running a blog is free or inexpensive and it's fairly easy to do through such providers as Blogger.com or Wordpress.com.

The blogging world (a.k.a. the blogosphere) can help you, the savvy job hunter, by making available numerous platforms wherein you can learn from the experiences, ideas, and insights of others in the job-hunting process. And in this process, up-to-date knowledge is key. Does having a career, job-hunting, or interviewing blog automatically make someone an expert in that area? No. Thus, you must sift through the blogosphere and find those that are professional, intelligent, and commonsensical. Quality varies widely, but here are a half dozen blogs to help get you started:

➧ CareerHub

➧ ResumeBear

➧ Careerealism

➧ Life After College

➧ The Undercover Recruiter

➧ The Daily Muse

If you are thinking about launching your own blog to raise your profile in an area such as the trials and tribulations of the modern job hunter:

➧ Scour the dozens of providers and thousands of blogs on the Web for positive role models before starting your own.

➧ Have something worthwhile to say.

➧ Be open to accepting feedback, both positive and negative.

➧ Be willing to invest the time and energy to post updates regularly to grow your follower base.

Wikis

Think of an electronic bulletin board where you can post information to be read, commented upon, or added to (a la Wikipedia) by a restricted population, and you've got a pretty good idea of what a wiki is. Because it is not open to the entire Internet, it is great for teams or task forces that share proprietary information; it may eventually make the traditional conference call obsolete. Setting up and running a wiki requires more Web know-how than a blog, so it is not for the novice, may require its own server, and should be run behind the corporate firewall. Do you want to learn more about wikis? Check out Wikihow.com (try the Work World category) and you'll see how diverse, but potentially time-wasting, the wiki world can be.

Webinars

Just as it sounds, a Webinar is a seminar conducted on the Web. It may be one-way, where you sit at your computer and listen, similar to a Webcast; or interactive, with capability for multiple presenters and/or questions and answers. It may be live or pre-recorded. It may be free, or you may be required to pay a fee to participate. Presenting or facilitating a quality Webinar is a good way of establishing your expertise in a field, and "attending" a Webinar may be a good way to quickly acquire information you need. I must caution you here that some free Webinars are little more than infomercials, and there is almost no quality control or reference data on the Webinars that cost money, so one is often reduced to, as the old saying goes, "buying a pig in a poke."

A Few Misconceptions about Job Hunting and Social Media

1. It can get me a job.
   Wrong—it can only *help* you get a job.
2. Social media is a fad.
   Wrong—it is a permanent and growing part of the job-hunting landscape.
3. Instant communication means instant results.
   Wrong—it may speed things up a bit, but the job-hunting process still takes longer than you ever feared it would.
4. I don't need social media because I'm already well-known in my field.
   Wrong—in five years, the percentage of employers using social media to recruit or research job candidates has grown from 78 percent to 94 percent. If you are not on social media, you are all but invisible. Even worse, it makes you look old, out of touch, and out of date. Worse still, if you are not defining yourself on social media, someone else might be.

Obvious and Not-So-Obvious Social Media Job-Hunting Mistakes

There are a deadly dozen common social networking mistakes that can have disastrous effects on your job hunt and career. They are:

1. Being invisible; not having a profile anywhere.

2. Not knowing what you look like on social media. Google yourself and review all your profiles.

3. Not removing objectionable or unprofessional material. If this is impossible, have a rationale/explanation for the interviewers who see it—and they will.

4. Not using the available privacy settings to keep private material private.

5. Being indiscreet; speaking ill of a former employer, boss, or colleague.

6. Having ungrammatical, misspelled, or angry, unpleasant posts.

7. Using social media while at work or on your employer's computer. You will be found out.

8. Having a profile that is inconsistent or inaccurate. Sure, you can sometimes fudge some titles a bit, but accomplishments, name of employers, dates, and degrees all need to be verifiable and in synch across various sites.

9. Only having a "print" resume or only an HTML resume. You need both. Some sites require your resume to be in an HTML format; others prohibit it. Dozens of Websites give you formats and show you how to prepare either.

10. Not making the effort to expand your online network. Adding a person a day is a minimal goal.

11. Oversharing/undersharing. Nobody needs to know every little thing about you or your career. On the other hand, this isn't the time to be modest about your strengths and accomplishments. Seek feedback you trust to help you find the right balance.

12. Spending too much or too little job-hunting time online. The vast array of electronic and Web-based tools out there can

be overwhelming. Consider using my 10–20–70 formula for apportioning your job-hunting time and energy. I advise you to invest:

➻ 10 percent of your time pursuing all forms of published openings (print and electronic).

➻ 20 percent of your time identifying (from your contacts and via the Web) and working with recruiters.

➻ 70 percent of your time networking (both in person and via the Web).

There is no specific formula that is perfect for everyone. As your search progresses, you can use your incoming results to adjust your overall strategy.

Any of the electronic tools, Websites, and social media we've covered in this section can be a significant boost to your job search. Taken together, they can markedly increase the effectiveness of any job search, reduce the amount of time it takes to uncover job leads, and, ultimately, help you land a good job. But none of them is perfect. Each has its own unique strengths and limitations, and I have tried to be even-handed about both.

These recently developed tools and innovative approaches reinforce the idea that the best use of the Web (for job hunters and non-job hunters alike) is to facilitate communication between people. This has been an essential requirement of the job search process for the last hundred years, and irrespective of any new and exciting technological development, it will be an essential requirement of the job search process for the next hundred years.

Master the Proven Four-Front Job Campaign

You now have a realistic set of goals for your job hunt, and you now know how to use the complete array of job-hunting methods to effectively identify your job targets. What you need next is a road map, a game plan, to help you put it all together. I like the phrase *job campaign*, because just like a military or political campaign, every activity is clearly linked to a specific, desired end result: you landing a great, new job.

Some job hunters start off by focusing on that one job-hunting method that was successful for them in their last job search. If a published opening or a Website worked last time, they spend most of their job-hunting time looking there. If a headhunter helped them last time, they call him or her and sit back waiting for the phone to ring. This is understandable, because if that method worked for you once, it was 100-percent successful—odds any job hunter would love.

Other job hunters, after reading a book like this one, will apportion their time and energy according to the general statistics of success for the various methods—for example, spending about 65 to 70 percent of their time networking, 15 to 20 percent of their effort working with re-cruiters, 10 to 15 percent of their energy cold-contacting potential em-ployers, and 5 to 10 percent of their time tracking down published open-ings. This approach appeals to the systems folks among us, but I find it's best to remember Mark Twain's comment, "There are lies, damned lies, and statistics." I suggest that you consider instead the 10–20–70 formula that combines both the traditional and Web-based approaches outlined earlier in this chapter.

I have found that some job hunters will concentrate their time and energy using the single job-hunting method with which they feel most comfortable: in the library, on the phone calling recruiters, out there networking, in church lighting candles.

For most job hunters, and especially at the initial stage of your job hunt, this approach is *dead wrong*!

The fact is that you have no objective data about what job-hunting method will be successful for you during *this* job campaign. Since the time of your last job hunt, you have changed, the job market has changed, employers have changed, recruiters have changed, useful Websites have changed, libraries have changed, the technology of your job has changed—everything is different. What guided you to success last time may or may not work for you this time. That is why you need to start off your job campaign with approximately equal energy on all four fronts.

Use Real-Time Feedback to Customize Your Job Hunt

Your job hunt is not a one-size-fits-all deal. It needs to be tailored to what you're qualified to do, what you are looking for, and where you are looking for it. After a month or two of pushing your job campaign on all four fronts, you will begin to see what is working for you at this point in your career. You should begin to reapportion your time and energy accordingly. If your current skill set is now attracting more recruiters, spend a little more time with them. Similarly, if your specific industry or function is now publicly posting/publishing more job openings, it makes sense to spend more of your time chasing down those leads. But you must not abandon the other fronts in your campaign. To understand why, take a look at Figure 3.1 on the next page.

This diagram gives a good, brief overview of the job-hunting process: you use various methods to uncover potential job leads; when you find out there is a bona fide job opening, you enter the screening process; if there is a potential fit, you may be screened by phone; if that goes well, you may get into the interview process; if your interview(s) goes well, your references may be checked; next, you may get a job offer; if you negotiate effectively, you may get an even better offer.

However, if you want to get some real insight into what the job-hunting process is like, show this diagram to someone currently hard at work on a job hunt. She will tell you that this illustration shows only a few of the ways a potentially good job lead can go south. Even with all the no's you see, it doesn't show the mail that wasn't delivered; it doesn't show the e-mail that got bounced; it doesn't show the day your voice mail failed and you missed that important call; it doesn't show when you went to the wrong place for the interview or you ended up interviewing with the wrong person, or the right interviewer turned out to be an idiot, or the time you gave references who were not sufficiently prepared or who decided to waste time telling all those funny stories about you, or the time, after you spent weeks doing everything right, they decided you were overqualified or too expensive, or the time when, for unknown reasons, the job you wanted so badly suddenly just went away. This is what a seasoned job hunter will tell you about the job-hunting process, which leads to my next point.

More Is Better

Job hunting is damn hard, it's unpredictable, and it can be very discouraging. But by understanding and managing the process, you can master it. This means you must continually use all job-hunting tools and avenues at your disposal. Using only one or two job-hunting methods will make your job campaign harder and longer. Look again at Figure 3.1. If you want to succeed at this process with the least amount of stress and strain possible, you must continuously use all four major job-hunting methods to *front-end load the system*. More contacts are better, more job

Job-Hunt Overview

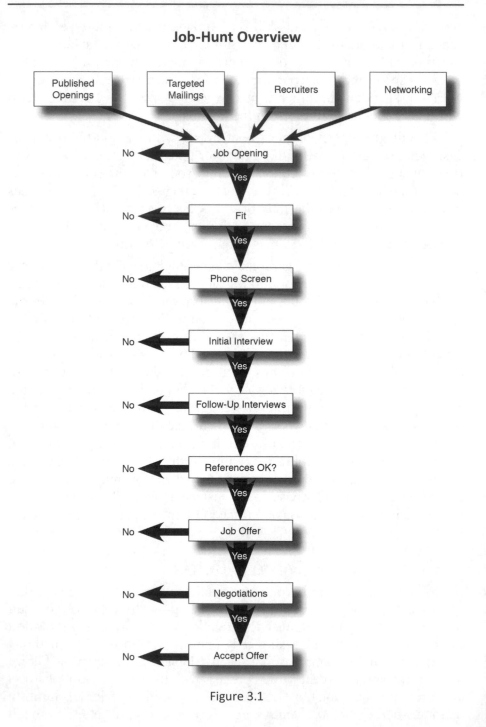

Figure 3.1

leads are better, more phone screens are better, more interviews are better, and more offers are better. In the job-hunting process, *more is always better.* With more input, there will be more output. It's as simple as that.

Never Stop Starting

There is another common job-hunting mistake I want you to avoid. It is easy, especially if you've been at it for a while, to get overexcited about a particular job opportunity you uncover. It's with a great company, and you've heard from your contact inside the organization that it's a great place to work. You have passed the screening phase and are now ready to begin the interview process. You feel in your bones that this could be the one. Nothing is more typical than, at this point, putting all your eggs in one basket. I mean this in two ways: operationally and emotionally.

Realistically, you must face the fact that this job may or may not happen. Even if you are the greatest job hunter in the world, have the best interviewing skills in the world, and are, in fact, the best candidate for the job, there are tons of reasons why it might not happen. Thus, you must *never* stop starting the process. The more spadework you do to front-end-load the job-hunting process, the better shape you will be in, operationally and emotionally, if one particular job doesn't pan out.

Even if you are going in for what you hope is your final interview, even if you already have an offer in hand, never stop starting. If this opportunity works out, that's great. You will sound more confident and maybe less willing to take whatever is offered to you because you have other opportunities in the pipeline. If this job falls through, at least you won't have lost a lot of time that keeping your job hunt moving forward.

Take one more look at Figure 3.1. How would you feel if you uncovered only one job lead at a time, pursued it through the process up to a point where you didn't get it, and then had to go back to square one and start from scratch? You'd feel lousy—disappointed, discouraged, maybe hurt or angry, and certainly demotivated. This is a recipe for job-hunting failure if ever there was one. Now think about going through this process a bunch of times. You'd be lucky to even get out of bed in the morning without thinking about jumping in front of a bus! One way to protect yourself emotionally during this process (which, as you remember from Chapter 1, is essentially a process of rejection) is to always be working on something new, always have something else in the pipeline. You must never stop starting—until after you have started your new job.

➤➤ ➤➤ ➤➤

Some of what we've discussed thus far hasn't exactly been all sweetness and light. Job hunting is a darn hard job—we all know that. Done correctly, it's a lot of work to get out there and conduct an effective, four-front job campaign to line up more and better interviews. But what comes next is where the tide turns in your favor. In Chapter 4 we're going to look at the most important person in the process—you. And we're going to talk about the control and power you have over this process, why you are in the driver's seat, and how you can use this knowledge to your best advantage.

Chapter 4

You're in the Driver's Seat

THE JOB-CHANGING PROCESS IS ONE BIG LEARNING EXPERIENCE. You will learn what has changed in the marketplace since the last time you searched for a job. You will learn what particular skills and experiences are now most in demand by employers in your field and function. You will learn about all the new and interesting ways to use social media to uncover job openings and expand your network of contacts. And you will learn that it is *you* who is driving the entire process, and that includes the all-important interview.

One of the most important things you can learn about job interviewing is that you—yes, that's right, *you*—can exercise a remarkable degree of control over the entire process. Understanding, using, and expanding on the control you have over the interview may be the single most important factor in your ability to get the job you want and build it into a job you can love.

You may say, "Nonsense. After all, *they* read my letter or e-mail, *they* screened my resume, *they* listened to the headhunter, *they* talked to the person who referred me, and, ultimately, *they* called me to come in for an interview at *their* location and at a time of *their* preference. And, oh, by the way, *they* will be asking the questions, *they* will determine if I'm the best job candidate, and *they* will decide if and when to make me a job offer. Exactly how does that put *me* in control?"

I wish I could tell you that I'm about to teach you the secret of the Vulcan mind meld so you could open up the interviewer's mind like a ripe melon, pluck out whatever you wanted, and bend him to your every whim. If I ever figure that one out, I'll let you know. But until then, you will have to be satisfied with the proven techniques and approaches I have learned from thousands of successful job hunters who have used them to take charge of their job interviews and land a job they love.

Why Control Is Important to You

Some folks just attract other people. I'm not talking about physical attractiveness here; I'm talking about personal traits such as friendliness, courtesy, genuine interest in the other person, good listening skills, and an ability to influence the environment rather than being driven or controlled by it. These qualities are essential to improving your interview performance.

A person who radiates a sense of control communicates competency, calm, and confidence. Your interviewing goal is to communicate that you are the best person for the job in question, and all three of these traits are essential to that goal.

A person who goes into an interview with a sense of control contributes to a climate of certainty, predictability, and lowered risk. These are subtle qualities all interviewers find attractive (though many don't even know it). Someone who feels out of control seems passive, not active; more of a follower than a leader; someone who doesn't stand out from the crowd.

No matter how subtly you feel it, a sense of powerlessness will work against you in your interview. When you feel out of control, it does not help you present yourself, either personally or professionally, in a way that attracts other people. And all of these factors are essential for you to deal with if you want to emerge from that interview as the leading job candidate.

Now, let's put the list together: you need to be competent, confident, certain, predictable, action-oriented, and attractive on both a personal and professional level. These are the very qualities that will lead you to winning job interviews and which will ensure your success in your new job. Here's how you get them.

Communicating Control

By "taking control" I do not mean charging into the interviewer's office like a star from the World Wrestling Federation, physically overwhelming the space with your body language and cologne while verbally dominating the conversation by not letting the interviewer get a word in edgewise. It might be kind of fun to watch, but it sure as heck won't get you the job.

It has been stated—and with some fairness, I think—that what is seen as legitimate assertiveness in some men can be seen as aggressiveness in some women. You've heard it all before, I'm sure. He's "take charge"; she's "bossy." He "looks out for his people"; she's "territorial." He can be a "pain in the neck"; she's a "pain in the..."—well, you get the picture. In an increasingly diverse working world, these attitudes may seem Neanderthal to you and me both, but my counsel is to ignore them at your peril.

Two things I am absolutely certain about are that (a) you *do* want to exhibit the appropriate level of assertiveness in the interview in order to demonstrate that you can completely fulfill the requirements of the job you're seeking, and (b) you *do not* want to cross the invisible (and sometimes gender-biased) line between assertiveness and aggression. There are three steps to managing this balancing act. They are: get smart, get feedback, and get ahead.

Get Smart

Women's and men's conversational styles differ in many ways, and how we converse with each other at work is how we get stuff done—planning, cooperating, coaching, directing, selling, disciplining, and leading. Improving your interpersonal communication style and understanding how others may perceive you are essential skills in today's world of work. Our conversational skills are constantly being evaluated at work and are scrutinized minutely under a microscope during the job-interview process.

Resources abound to help you increase your knowledge and skills of communication. Regarding gender differences in communication, I strongly recommend the now-classic book *Talking From 9 to 5: How*

Women's and Men's Conversational Styles Affect Who Gets Heard, Who Gets Credit, and What Gets Done at Work (William Morrow, 1994), by Dr. Deborah Tannen, who is a leader in this field. Dr. Tannen has had other best-sellers on this topic, but this one is a must for the bookshelf of any manager or job hunter.

My next recommendation might surprise you a little bit. One of the best general texts I've found on how to improve your communication skills is another classic titled *How to Talk So Kids Will Listen and Listen So Kids Will Talk* (Perennial Currents, 1999), by Adele Faber and Elaine Mazlish. I've had a number of clients tell me that Faber and Mazlish's ideas for improving their listening and understanding skills, dealing with feelings, and encouraging both autonomy and cooperation are just as useful at work as they are at home. Communication skills that make you a winner at work are certain to make you irresistible as a job candidate. Thus, making the effort to improve your skills in this area will generate concrete benefits during this and every other stage of your career.

Get Feedback

The problem with any book is that it is one-way communication. I can talk to you, but you can't talk back to me (at least not in any way I can hear). I have no effective way of assessing your communication style, whether it is too loud or too soft, too laid back or too domineering, too indirect or too in your face. I have no way of offering you remedial actions or improvement ideas. You need real feedback, and here's how to get it:

1. Take a moment to look at the Energy Level/Communication Effectiveness Model in Figure 4.1 on the next page. It shows how communicating with too much or too little energy can negatively affect how you communicate.

2. Because you are one of the best sources of information about yourself, ask yourself the following questions:
   a. When do I communicate in the passive zone?
   b. When do I communicate in the assertive zone?
   c. When do I communicate in the aggressive zone?
   d. In what zone do I most frequently communicate?
   e. In what zone do I most frequently communicate when I'm interviewing?

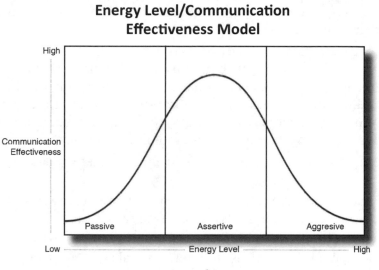

Figure 4.1

3. Find some other sources of feedback. Ask a couple of trusted (and honest!) friends or colleagues the same five questions you asked yourself in number 2. Search your old performance reviews for clues. Who else has data you could gather, who else knows you well—a mentor, a counselor, a former coworker?

4. Write down these impressions and see how they coincide or conflict with your self-assessment. Finally, compile an overall assessment of the energy level you most frequently use when communicating.

Get Ahead

If you have determined that you are predominantly a passive or an aggressive communicator, you will need to make some major changes. Not to worry—very few people are born with precisely fine-tuned communication skills, and there are many readily available steps you can take if you really want to develop winning job interview skills.

Let's say you have figured out that you are too passive in the way you communicate with others. This is bad news because no job interviewer is going to sit there and try to pry information out of you. He might think you're not overly interested in the job, not "good with people," painfully shy, hung over, or who knows what else. In any event, you will not stand out as a great interviewer.

On the other hand, maybe you have determined that you are much too aggressive in the way you communicate with others. This is also bad news because you will be seen as hard to work with, a know-it-all, not a team player, or domineering. No interviewer is going to recommend hiring you if you come off as an angry, opinionated loudmouth, unless you're looking for a job as a wing-nut radio talk show host.

If you want to improve your skills in either of these areas, here are a few ideas you can use:

➥   See if your current employer offers any in-house workshops in communication skills or assertiveness training.

➥   Go to your human resources department and see what information they have about interpersonal skills workshops or assertiveness training seminars offered locally. Find out if your employer will pay for all or part of it. Many do.

➥   Call your local community college and look up what adult education courses or workshops they offer in this area; tuition is often very low, and you can either use it as a tax deduction, or your employer may reimburse you.

➥   Use the Internet to find your local Toastmasters International chapter (*www.toastmasters.org*). Start attending their meetings, and I guarantee that you'll enjoy the fellowship you experience while you build your communication skills.

Whose Interview Is It, Anyway?

I want you to actually stop for a minute or two to think about this question. Sure, your potential employer is interviewing you, but she is probably interviewing other folks, as well. This makes the time you are there *your* interview. It's *your* time to sell your skills and background, it's *your* time to be seen as a winner, and it's *your* time to shine. This interview is *yours*, and I want you to take responsibility for it.

I don't care if you're being interviewed by the biggest dope on the planet; you can (subtly, of course) control the flow, the atmosphere, most of the content, and sometimes even the actual outcome of your job hunt by learning the interviewing secrets you'll find in this chapter. In more than 30 years of working as a psychologist in a variety of different settings (executive coach, outplacement consultant, executive recruiter, and career counselor), I've discovered how the most anxious, tentative job hunter can learn to be a great job interviewer.

By taking personal responsibility for your interview, you will start to assert control over it. And you will learn to take control of it by going into your interview with:

1. The right attitude.
2. The right knowledge of the process.
3. The right preparation.

We will cover attitude and knowledge now and devote the entire next chapter to preparation.

The Right Attitude

If you are a human being, your emotions affect how you behave. How you behave influences how others around you behave. Thus, going into your job interview with the right attitude can affect how you behave and how the interviewer behaves, and will influence the outcome of the interview. If you go into an interview with a hat-in-hand attitude or a "please sir, I need this job" attitude, you will undercut the positive impression you're trying to make. However, if you go into your interview with an upbeat, "this is a great opportunity for both of us" attitude, you will make a much stronger and more positive impression of yourself as a person and of your professional capabilities. We have already touched on one way for you to develop the right interviewing attitude, that is, by understanding whose interview this is, by knowing who owns this interview—you. Let's look at a few more ways to make this happen.

The Wind Is in Your Favor

You have psychology working for you because the interviewer assumes, more or less, that you can do the job. That's right! You're not going in as a blank slate; you're going in with an assumption in your favor. In today's hectic world, no one has the spare time to interview someone whom they think *can't* do the job, do they? Only the best candidates, only the most appropriately skilled individuals, only those folks whom the interviewer actually *hopes* can do the job are being interviewed. Of course, it's up to you to support the assumption that you actually *can* do the job, but in reality, the interviewer is already part of the way there.

This Isn't *Law & Order*

The interview is a two-way street. You're not going in to be grilled like a hot dog on the Fourth of July, nor are you going to be subjected to "advanced interrogation techniques" in sunny Guantanamo Bay. (On a rare occasion, you may run into some moron who thinks he'll run you through a stress interview. Don't worry about that for now. We'll cover that later, in Chapter 9.) You are going in for a business meeting, one where business information is sought and offered on a two-way street. They have work that needs to be done and the money to pay for it. You have the skills and attitude to get that job done. They are trying to determine if you are the best person for them, and you are trying to find out if this is the best place for you to work at this point in your career. A good interview is a professional meeting to determine whether two parties can come to an agreement in their mutual best interest. It is not a situation in which one side has all the power.

You Have a Real Edge

You probably know more about the interviewing process than the interviewer does. If you read this book from cover to cover and learn only half of what I've put in here for you, you will still have a better handle on the interviewing process than 90 percent of the interviewers you will run into. Eight nationwide corporate training firms recently verified what I have discovered in my own consulting practice: one of the least-attended management training courses or seminars are those on interviewing skills for hiring managers. I'm told the reason is that most hiring managers have been interviewed themselves on any number of occasions, so they think they know how to do a good job at it. I'm here to tell you that most of them do a lousy job of interviewing. This is bad news for most companies but good news for you, because I'm going to teach you what they don't know, and what they don't know will help you knock that interview out of the park.

It's Like Skydiving

In job interviewing (like skydiving), you don't get a do-over if you blow it on the first try. You never get a second chance to make a first impression. So, how do you go into an interview—often a first meeting—and have it look and feel as if you're a seasoned, comfortable professional? The answer is by thorough preparation and leaving nothing to chance.

Preparing for the interview will immeasurably improve your attitude, build your confidence, and enhance the way you present yourself. Because this is so important, we will spend an entire chapter on the easy-to-follow steps that you can take to prepare effectively for your interview. (Unfortunately, most job candidates' preparation for a job interview consists of getting a good night's sleep.) But for now, the very fact that you take the time to actively prepare for the interview means that you will go into it with more poise, more thoughtfulness, and more confidence—a winning combination if ever there was one.

Why Are You There?

I want you to walk into that interview knowing exactly why you are there. Having a crystal-clear goal foremost in your mind will improve your interviewing attitude immensely. If the interview is a screening interview, your goal is to get called back for the next step in the hiring process. If it is a group interview, your goal is to personally connect with as many people in the group as possible. If it is a final interview, your goal is to close the deal and get the job offer. Most people go into an interview with the idea that they will see what happens or hope for the best. Not you. With my help, you're going in to win!

The Right Knowledge

Knowledge is power, in interviewing as well as in the rest of life. In the job interview the interviewer discovers things about you—details about your education, your working relationships, your previous assignments, and your career aspirations. It is not, however, the correct venue for you to be discovering basic things—either about the organization with the job opening or about the interview process itself.

That is all knowledge you should have brought to the interview with you, to help you tailor your answers and your follow-up questions, and to improve your overall presentation. Sure, you should be in there actively listening and picking up on new information, but you shouldn't be in there in basic research mode. I don't want you in there trying to find out stuff your competition already knows. I want you in there sharing new ideas, explaining how you plan to contribute—essentially selling yourself. I want you walking into that interview knowing more about your potential employer than all the other candidates do. I also want you walking into the interview better prepared than all the other candidates by completely understanding the dynamics of the interview process itself. By doing these things, you will walk out of the interview a winner.

Back to Your New Best Friend

In the last chapter I introduced you to your new best friend, your reference librarian. Not only can this person help you in setting your overall job hunting goals, but he will also be invaluable in the critical phase of interview preparation.

You want to arrive for an interview with a boatload of information. What do you know about the organization where you are asking to spend months and maybe years of your life? What do you know about its products or services? What do you know about its reputation, its history, its various locations, and its financial health? Why is this job open? What challenges do you think will face the person who fills this job opening? These are only a few of the questions you should be asking yourself before you present yourself for the interview.

Having answers to all of these questions will help distinguish you from the other job candidates during the interview process in a number of very important ways.

- The most obvious benefit is that by knowing more about the organization, you are better equipped to sell yourself into it by matching your skills with its needs.
- By knowing more about the organization, you can more easily establish a common vocabulary with the interviewer, and that facilitates the overall level of communication.
- You will demonstrate that the job-hunting and interviewing process is of prime importance to you and that you are willing to invest the time and energy to succeed at it.
- You will subtly communicate that you are hardworking, serious, thorough, and curious—not to mention knowledgeable.

These are qualities every potential employer is looking for, and demonstrating them will put you in the top tier of job candidates.

You also want to learn as much as you can about the interviewer himself. Any common ground you can find will help you, especially during those first awkward stages of establishing a relationship. Do you know any people in common? Has anyone in your network ever met or worked with this person? Do you belong to any organizations in common? Has he ever made any presentations that you can access, or has he written anything you can read? Have you Googled the interviewer to see what else there might be to learn or checked him out via his various profiles on social media? An obvious (I hope) caution here is to use any personal information that you uncover judiciously, because nobody wants to hire a stalker!

Pick up on the Rhythm

Every interview has a predictable rhythm. Understanding this rhythm is easy once you are aware of it. It will give you valuable feedback (during the interview itself) that will help you know how you are doing and help you get a better sense of where you are in the process. You can use this knowledge to fine-tune your approach even as the interview is underway. Let's take a quick look at Figure 4.2.

Interview Process Overview

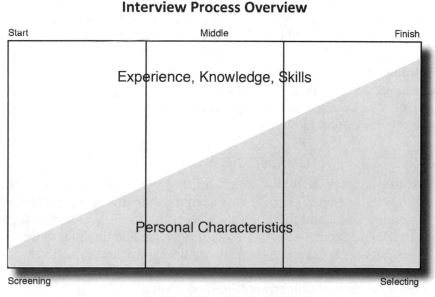

Figure 4.2

This model gives you an easy way to look at two important aspects of job interviewing. The top line goes from start through middle to finish. This represents the progress you make going through an individual interview. The bottom line goes from the screening phase to the selecting phase. This represents where you are in the overall interview process. Note that both ends of the interview process explore the same issues but in very different proportions.

As an organization begins to evaluate you during the screening process, it needs to confirm that you and the other candidates the organization plans to invite for interviews can, in fact, do the job. That means verifying that you have the experience, skills, and knowledge to do the job. To figure out if you are still in the screening process or if you have moved forward to the selection process, just consider the questions you are asked on the phone or in person. If the focus is primarily on experience, skills, and knowledge, you are still in the screening process. If the focus is heavily weighted on who you are as a person (your personal qualities, your family, your outside interests, and the like), you have moved on to the selection process.

This insight also helps you determine where you are in any individual interview. Most interviewers go into the process with an agenda; it might not be an organized one or a particularly effective one, but they usually have *some* basic game plan. After a few opening pleasantries, typically they will moved on to their agenda. Once they have learned what they needed to know, they will often move on to softer, more personal questions that focus on who you are as a person. You need to observe this process closely, because these questions can give you important information as to how you are doing and can give strong clues as to exactly what it is they are looking for.

You Can See the Future

If I've heard it once, I've heard it hundreds of times. It's a nervous job interviewee saying that she hates being put on the spot, that she's not very spontaneous, and that she can never think of the best way to answer questions when she's under pressure. If only she had the interviewer's list of questions ahead of time; then she could calmly and reflectively come up with the best, most interesting way to portray her background. She wouldn't be floundering around in the hot seat.

Some think I've blown a gasket when I tell them that they have at their disposal a tool that will predict 80 to 90 percent of the interview questions they will ever be asked. They really start to wonder when I say that this tool, at this very moment, is somewhere on their desk or in their briefcase or in the job-search folder in their computer. Can you guess what this secret weapon is?

This secret weapon is your updated resume. You have written your resume so that it highlights all the great things you've done, all your accomplishments, all the wonderful stuff you want to talk about. (I mean, nobody's resume has negative stuff on it such as "Rolled the delivery van, cost the company $150,000 in a lawsuit.") Your resume is a sequential roadmap through all the places you've worked. It details all your relevant education and training. In short, it has tons of positive information that you want your interviewer to hear.

Your resume presents you with a golden opportunity to put an interview outline you have designed, with data you have chosen and want to be asked about, directly into the hands of your interviewer. The key to using this secret weapon is to know this information in complete detail—backward and forward and inside out.

Sure, a few questions may come from left field, but most of them will stay pretty darn close to the data you have chosen to present, and (here's more good news) you will have had all the stress-free time in the world before the interview to come up with accurate and insightful answers to any of them.

Turning Good Into Great

In the next chapter we'll delve more deeply into preparing specific answers to questions. What I'd like you to do now is set some really high expectations for your interviews. I don't want them to be just good; I want them to be great. When you walk out of the interviewer's office, I want him to say, "Boy, I enjoyed that. What an interesting person. I hope we can get her to work here." Here's one way to turn good interviews into great interviews.

I want you to take each little item on your resume—that's *every* item—and justify why it's there. It should say something great about you. If it's boring, edit it out. If it highlights one of your strengths, it's in. Then, for every remaining resume item, I want you to come up with an interesting story about it. Dry facts don't sell. Interesting, engaging stories sell. You want to fill your interview with engaging, interesting stories that highlight all the wonderful things you can bring to a new employer. Regardless of one's religious beliefs, it's easy to see that Jesus' ability to tell powerful but simple stories (called *parables*) about the most basic things in life is one of the reasons that a tiny sect grew into one of the most powerful movements the world has ever known. Now, I'm not expecting you to convert the world. I just want you to bring a few interviewers into your flock.

Your Fail-Safe Backup Plan

You, my astute job candidate, may ask, "Okay, so I can predict most of the questions I'll be asked. What about the 10 to 20 percent that I can't predict?" We're not talking about doofus questions here. (Occasionally, you may get the whacko who asks who your favorite kid in the *Brady Bunch* was. We'll have some fun with the topic of idiot interviewers in Chapter 9.) I'm talking about a question that clearly relates to the job you're hoping to land but somehow you didn't see coming. Not to worry. Dr. Paul has a fail-safe answer for you, and it's a great one at that. All you have to do is understand and remember the equation in Figure 4.3. It is with great pride that I can say for decades successful job candidates have told me that learning (and remembering to use) my unique formula for a fail-safe interview answer was one of the most important factors in lowering their interview stress and contributing to their interview success.

Dr. Paul's Fail-Safe
Interview Answer Formula

$$[Ex + Kn] + [PC] = \text{Fail-Safe Answer}$$

Ex = Experience

Kn = Knowledge

PC = Personal Characteristics

Figure 4.3

Whether you know it or not, every interview question you are asked is actually a two-part question. The first part is the hard data: your experience, your knowledge, and your skills. It is designed to answer the question, "Can he or she do the job?" The second part is the soft data: your personal characteristics, your personality, and who you are as a person. How would you doing the job be different from anybody else doing the job? It is designed to answer the question, "Of all the qualified candidates, is she the one that fits best with the rest of the organization?" No matter what interview question you are asked, whether or not you have a prepared answer, you need to hit both of these chords. This is not only a fail-safe answer for an unexpected question, it is also another way to think about turning a good answer into a great answer for any question.

Part one (knowledge and experience) without part two (personal characteristics) gives an answer that is flat and impersonal. That answer will only tell how anybody would do the job if they had the right background; it doesn't help you stand out from the crowd. Part two (personal characteristics) without part one (knowledge and experience) is too generic and too vague; it doesn't address the basic issue of job performance that must be answered, and it will sound as if you're trying to sell yourself into a job for which you may not be qualified.

Using this easy-to-remember equation will help you generate a strong answer to any interview question, one that supplies the confirmation that you have the hands-on skills and background to do the job, as well as the personal qualities that make you an enjoyable teammate and someone with whom others will like to work. If you use it, you will never again be stumped by an interview question that seems to come out of left field.

➤➤ ➤➤ ➤➤

By now you have learned that the job interview belongs to you: it is yours to control, yours to win, or yours to blow. It is up to you to drive the interview in the direction you want. We have taken a look at two of the major ways you can take control of it: by developing the right attitude and by gaining essential knowledge of the process. Now you are ready to move on to Chapter 5, where I will show you an easy-to-follow plan that will help you prepare thoroughly and professionally for any interview and dramatically increase the odds that you will land the job you really want.

Chapter 5

Getting to the Short List

JOB HUNTING IS A COMPETITIVE ENDEAVOR. You will have others competing with you for the job you want at every step of the selection process. If you've been reading this book from front to back, you have already learned many techniques and shortcuts to help you separate yourself from the pack of other job candidates. Now we need to ramp up your energy, approach, and skills, and focus on getting you past the screening process and onto the short list of potential employees.

I have heard people refer to a job interview as an audition or a command performance. Some think that this belittles the process as something phony or, play acting as opposed to the serious business of landing a job you love. I do not.

Skilled performers don't just go out on stage to see what will happen next. They plan, they prepare, they practice, and they leave nothing to chance. Sure, there are some performers who improvise more than others (jazz musicians and other performers like the late, great Robin Williams come to mind), but even they are working with a plan, within a certain structure, and with a definite end point in mind. This is how

I want you to be prepared for your job interviews: relaxed but focused, prepared but not robotically programmed, ready to shine and with your eyes on the prize.

Anxiety and stress do indeed affect performance, but they are not bad things in and of themselves. As you learned in Chapter 2, they are the ways our bodies and our minds tell us that we are in a situation of some risk—a job interview, for example. In fact, a certain, moderate amount of stress can give you the extra edge (that is, heightened awareness, alertness, responsiveness) that can help you turn a good interview into a great interview. The exhilarated feeling you have after you've left an interview where you did really well is, in fact, adrenaline at work.

For many people, however, the anxiety and stress brought on by an interview can be a real problem. Some get so nervous that they forget basic, boilerplate information about themselves—such as their name! Or they get so tongue-tied that they can barely squeak out a yes or no answer. I want you to control, but not completely eliminate your interview anxiety. I want you comfortably relaxed, but not so chilled out that you come across as laissez-faire or uninterested. I still want you to maintain that edge, that look in your eye that says, "I know this is an important meeting and I'm up for it because I'm well prepared"—energized and confident, but not cocky. There are several ways to achieve this vital balance. Let's focus first on some of the practical and tactical issues that are so often overlooked.

Looking and Feeling Your Best

Professional, friendly, attractive, and comfortable—these four qualities should be the hallmarks of your personal presentation at your interview. They apply to your interview outfit, your shoes, your haircut, your mustache, beard, or goatee, your eyeglasses, your bag (purse or briefcase), your pad and pen, and anything else the interviewer can see. Remember, this person has only a limited amount of time (a few hours at best) to decide if he wants to spend some number of months or even years with you, so he is looking for any piece of data from which he can draw assumptions about you.

Your Arrival

Woody Allen once said that showing up is 80 percent of life. I think the number goes considerably higher if we're talking about job interviews.

There may be some uncertainties about your interview, but one thing we know for a fact is that it ain't gonna happen if you ain't there! You need to know exactly where your interview is, exactly how to get there, and exactly how long it will take to get there. One of the worst ways to start an interview is to come racing in the door, late, making excuses and offering apologies.

Don't rely on any single source of data to find the location of your interview. Call and ask the receptionist for directions and check that he or she is actually familiar with the route you will be taking. If you're using public transportation, talk to someone who is actually familiar with the system and knows the stops. If using directions downloaded from the Web, check more than one source, because as wonderful as these sites can be, they can also be off by as much as a hemisphere. Check the Website of the organization you're interviewing with to see if it has directions posted. (I have found these directions to be the most reliable.) If you have found your GPS to be accurate, use it. But because a job interview is so darn important, I'd review it ahead of time and compare the directions to at least one other source.

If practical, make a test run to your interview site. Do this at the same time of day as your interview. This is good data to have in the event that you are offered the position and you need to figure out how long your new commute will be. These points may seem minor now, but together they all will contribute to your looking, feeling, and doing your best in the interview.

Your Outfit

You need two or three interview outfits. Have an objective, professional friend give you some honest feedback about which of your outfits work best. (If you are working with a recruiter, she can give you some excellent input.) If you need to update your wardrobe, it's the cost of doing business. Just make sure to wear the outfits a few times to break them in before your interview. You don't want a stray pin, dangling thread, pinching underwire, or scratchy label making you twitch around in your seat. This goes double for new shoes that may squeak, slip, or make you walk funny. Open-toed sandals, flip-flops, sneakers, or other sports shoes are all taboo.

Much has been made of the new, more casual look in the workplace. Because I truly believe that neckties are tools of the devil (and I'm told pantyhose are, as well), I'm all for the casual look. But the casual look is for people who are already *on the bus*. You are *not* on the bus—yet. The interview process is for them to see whether or not they *let you* on the bus. I don't care if the dress code at your potential new employer is Hawaiian shirts and bunny slippers. You show up for your interview dressed professionally. You can always remove your jacket or loosen your tie if asked to, but you want to communicate that this is an important enough meeting for you to do whatever it takes to make a positive impression.

Once you're comfortable with your interview outfits, have them cleaned and pressed, and keep them separate from the rest of your clothes. You want to have them ready to go at the drop of a hat in case you suddenly get that interview call you've been waiting for.

The Whole Pantyhose and Flip-Flop Thing

A couple of years ago I was delivering a talk (motivational, I hope) to a job-hunters' networking group. It was on a Wednesday morning, so I was pretty darn sure everybody there was unemployed. During the Q&A session, someone asked a question about interview attire. I made many of the points I'm making here in this chapter. I also advised against anything that might be considered provocative, such as shirts that show your belly or your cleavage, shorts, skirts that are too tight or too short, and any aspect of your underwear. A woman in the crowd took exception to my comments and in appreciation of my volunteering a half-day of my time to help them with their job searches, she indicated that she thought my comments were outdated, parochial, and sexist. As any professional speaker would, I tried to lighten the moment by confessing that yes, indeed, I had gone to parochial school but I didn't expect anyone to dress like a nun, though I did feel compelled to also advise against patent leather shoes. Most in the crowd chuckled. (If the patent leather shoe joke makes no sense to you, ask any survivor of a parochial school dance.)

Unfortunately, the group's laughter really set this angry lady off and she went into a tirade about pantyhose and bra straps and camisoles and men getting away with ogling. I'm pretty sure I had not come out in favor of ogling, but whatever. I again tried to lighten the mood and said that everything I knew about pantyhose was based on second-hand information and if pantyhose was such a big problem, then there are plenty of women's business suits with slacks. In retrospect, that would have been a good place to stop. But it hadn't yet dawned on me that the group's laughter was revving this poor woman up even more, so I mentioned that in the event I was coaching a man who wore women's undergarments, I would also suggest that he make an effort to conceal them. With her still wagging her finger at me, I tried to close this discussion with the generalization about making a professional versus a social impression and that, at work, a classic look always beats out trendy. Her final salvo was, "You mean I shouldn't wear flip-flops even if it was for a job modeling flip-flops?" I was at the end of my rope and my patience and said, "I'm not sure that flip-flop modeling jobs even exist, but if I was interviewing someone for that job, I hope that he or she would arrive with clean feet in clean socks in clean shoes." So, quibble with any point you want; it's no big whoop to me. I've got a job. It's you getting a job that I'm concerned with here and my 30-plus years' experience in this field supports every suggestion made in this book.

Your Grooming

This quick section should almost go without mention. Almost. Except that I've seen people show up for interviews with haircuts that look like they were done by a blender. I've been told of senior managers who showed up for interviews smelling as if they had been held hostage for a month in a garlic warehouse. And, on one occasion, I actually had to open a window so I wouldn't gag on petroleum fumes because this executive had spilled gasoline all over his shoes at a self-service station on his way to my office. (For Pete's sake, either pump your gas the day before or find a place where they'll pump it for you!) Do any of these single idiosyncrasies mean that the candidate cannot do the job? No. Can any of these single idiosyncrasies stick in an interviewer's head and ultimately work against the candidate? Yes. Sorry, pal, I didn't make up these rules; I'm just trying to help you win by understanding them.

Men: You don't need a manicure, but do invest in a nailbrush and clippers.

Women: Your job interview isn't the time or place to test-drive that new *Star Wars* makeup kit.

Haircut rules: Neat, presentable, and in a color frequently associated with human beings. This is not the time to make a fashion statement unless the statement is, "I'm great, I'm normal, please hire me."

You can't walk down a city street (or watch an NBA game) these days without noticing the growing number of tattoos, piercings, nose rings, and other body art. A trip to some beaches is even scarier. My advice is:

if you have this stuff, keep it covered or remove it when interviewing, because it can work against you. If you are hired, you can gradually start displaying, safety-pinning, or clipping on whatever you choose—at least until someone complains to the boss. There are alternative workplaces (such as bars, music stores, entertainment venues, and such) where body art is a nonissue. But most organizations that deal with the public or work with other businesses aren't that interested in hiring someone who looks as if he's been rolling around in a tackle box or would set off a TSA metal detector. Some organizations now have policies governing tattoos, piercings, and the like. If this is where you want to make your big existential stand and say, "This is how I am, they can hire me or not," then so be it. Just be clear that you might be trading off a paycheck for that nose ring.

Your Stuff

You don't want to trudge into the interview room burdened down with a bunch of stuff, making you look like a gold miner's pack mule. Stash your hat, coat, umbrella, galoshes, and change of shoes (if necessary) in a closet in the lobby or lunchroom. Try to find a rest room to comb your hair or give yourself a once-over.

One bag—that's it, that's all you bring in. There are some nice briefcases available that aren't all that expensive; if yours is beat up, go get a new one. Do not use your bike messenger bag or the grungy backpack that you take to the gym. If you are a woman, your briefcase will need to be a bit bigger to accommodate the essentials from your purse. This looks more professional than having a bag swinging from each shoulder like Gunga Din.

You need to have a pad of paper and a couple of working pens (no chew marks, please) with which you can take notes if you need to. You should have a couple of file folders: one with some extra copies of your resume and one with some copies of the list with your job references. If you are an artist or designer of some sort, you may need to have some portfolio pieces with you to show.

What Else?

Jewelry: Keep it to a minimum, nothing jangling or distracting.

Wristwatch: Something businesslike (no cartoon characters), with the alarm turned off.

Aftershave, cologne, or perfume: If you must, wear only the slightest hint, because many folks are allergic.

Breath mints: These are always a good idea, as is brushing your teeth (men—keep that stupid tie out of the sink).

Makeup: This isn't a fashion show or nightclub; subtle works best.

Eyeglasses: No shades or tinted lenses, and clean the leftovers from lunch off of the lenses.

Electronics: All turned off, off, off.

Your Smile

There is nothing more attractive than a smile. Books have been written, poems have been recited, songs have been sung, and hearts have been won and lost from the power of a smile. Practice one right now. Feels good, eh? Your smile is an invaluable tool that you must remember to take with you and use in your interviews.

I know that you're a little tense, you're hoping to do your best, and you're trying to remember all the great answers that you have so thoroughly prepared. But when most of us are deep in thought, we don't smile; we frown. You need to change this, and you can do it with practice. (We'll talk more about this later.)

When you smile at someone, the natural reaction is for him or her to return your smile. A smile is one of the very first building blocks in a relationship, and that's what you are trying to accomplish in your interview—to build a relationship with your interviewer. You want to communicate that you are an open, communicative, engaging, and willing partner in this process. Remembering to smile will help you immeasurably.

Your Attitude

When you arrive for your interview, I want you to have a positive, winning attitude. Smiling will help improve your attitude, but there's a little more work to do than just that. By making the effort to prepare thoroughly for your interview, you will have reduced your stress. By practicing your interviewing skills, you will have additionally eased your interview anxiety. What else can you do?

The answer to this question varies from person to person, and there is no one-size-fits-all answer. If you carry your stress in your body, exercise, such as a bike ride, a walk, or a jog, can help. If you tend to be a worrier or carry your anxiety around in your head, watching a movie, reading, reciting a prayer, or meditating can help. Maybe what will help you most is a combination of two or more different approaches. But choose some specific, positive activity to improve your interviewing attitude, because it is a key factor in how you will be perceived.

Questions and Answers

In Chapter 4, you learned some very important things about the questions you will be hearing in your job interviews. The vast majority of them can be answered with data that come right from your resume, which is why it is so important that you have a great resume and that you know it inside and out. Not all interviewers will have your resume in front of them. Some of the best interviewers I've ever seen make a list of their questions ahead of time on a separate piece of paper, and, assuming most of what is on your resume is genuine, put the resume away and only include one or two things from it that they want to explore in detail. If you find yourself in this situation, I want you to not just offer, but actually hand over one of the copies of your resume that you brought with you. Most interviewers will not decline it, and, with some luck, you're back to the situation where they are using the roadmap of your design as their map to your great job interview. Again, it is essential for you to have an interesting story to tell that illustrates every single item on that document.

In Chapter 4, you also learned that those questions that do not come directly from your resume can be answered with the judicious use of Dr. Paul's Fail-Safe Interview Answer Formula (Figure 4.3). There are dozens of questions that are asked time and time again. I have listed more than a hundred of the most popular ones for you in Tool #7: Frequently Asked Interview Questions, in Chapter 10. Ultimately, I want you to prepare answers for each of them and use them in your practice sessions. For now, the way to start is by taking the time to completely think through two things:

1. What is it that the interviewer is hoping to learn about you?
2. What is it that you want to make sure the interviewer learns about you?

Most of the time there is a great deal of overlap between these two areas. But in case the interviewer doesn't do a great job of discovering how wonderful you are, it is *up to you* to make sure this message gets across. These two categories could account for about a million different questions and answers, and there's no way anyone could ever prepare for them all. Fortunately, there is a tool that you can use to organize your interview preparation. Consider Figure 5.1. In the following sections, we'll talk through each of the circles shown here.

Interview Preparation

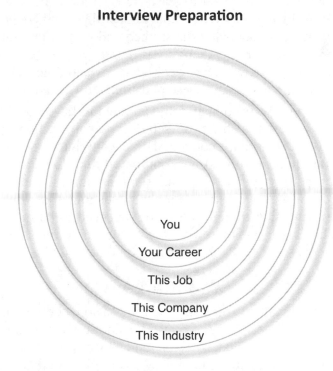

Figure 5.1

"I'll Take the Category *Hire Me* for 400, Alex"

My reading tastes are pretty eclectic, and, having a mind that retains tons of fun albeit pretty useless information, I once read a book by Alex Trebek about the TV show, *Jeopardy!* In it he mentions how some big *Jeopardy!* winners prepare themselves. They don't randomly read book after book or peruse the encyclopedia; instead, they take the time to think through which categories might appear and dig into them one by one (for example, mountain ranges, Shakespearean tragedies, and, my personal favorite, potent potables). Using this technique, we can successfully predict the categories of questions you will be asked, and you can systematically begin to organize your preparation for the interview itself.

You

Granted, this category is large. The way to narrow it down is to ask yourself what you would need to learn about a job candidate as an individual before hiring her. You would want to learn where she is from, where she went to school, what she studied and why, what motivates and demotivates her, what her personality is like, how she deals with stress, what her strengths are, what her weaknesses are, and how she will fit in with the rest of the team. And these questions only scratch the surface.

To out-prepare your competition, you need to have positive, insightful answers to questions about yourself as a person—who you are as an individual. But this is not enough. Should your interviewer gloss over this important area, you must have, prepared and up your sleeve, a list of your most positive personal qualities and attributes, and you must be able to find a way to work them into the questions that you *are* asked. You can't risk waiting to be discovered; you need to be in there selling yourself. This is just one more way you can get onto the short list of job candidates.

Your Career

We've already talked about your resume as an essential guide to your interview. You will get plenty of questions about why you did this, how you did that, why did you take this job, and why did you move to that job. Along these same lines, an astute interviewer will note that your resume details only the career choices that you actually made. She may ask about what other options you had, what paths you did not follow, what opportunities you missed, and what decisions you wish you could do over.

A good interviewer will not only want to learn about your career history, but he will want to know where you see your career going in the future. You should expect questions about your three-, five-, and perhaps 10-year goals, and how you see this job advancing your overall career plans. This can be tricky. You don't want to look like you're already planning to leave a job you don't yet have. On the other hand, you do want to give a sense that you are hoping to continue moving your career forward. Try out a few answers that sound and feel like you (not me). Some things to consider including are: what you hope to learn at your new job, wondering about what the possibility is of internal progress, and assuming that some new doors will appear and open for you as you succeed at this new job. No one can see the future, and you are not expected to be clairvoyant. What you need to communicate is a sense of purpose and direction.

This Job

You're not interviewing for just any job; you're interviewing for *this* job. Why do you want this job? It's a basic question, but you darn well better have a good answer for it. Historians note that this single interview question from newsman Roger Mudd torpedoed Ted Kennedy's quest for the U.S. presidency. You may not be running for political office, but I'd guess that this job you're interviewing for means more to your career and your family than anybody you'll ever vote for. A convincing response to why *this* job is the one for you will always stick in the interviewer's mind.

What have you learned about this job? Why is there an opening? What types of people succeed in this job? Who did it before? Where is she now? Is it a new position? What new opportunities does it represent? Your networking may have provided you with some of this information, the business press may have provided other information, and if you are working through a headhunter, she may have been able to give you some insight. Difficult though it may be, it is necessary to use all of your resources to gather pre-interview intelligence about the job for which you're interviewing.

This Company

When you go in for an interview, it is important that you demonstrate interest not only in the job, but also in the hiring organization. This type of preparation demonstrates to the interviewer that you are knowledgeable, thorough, and hardworking. A wealth of information is available about any organization. The key here is to allow yourself enough time before the interview to gather the information you need. You may be in the occasional situation in which, on the day before your interview, you are scrambling to build your data bank. Try to avoid this because, in your haste, you may miss an important piece of information. I hate to sound like your mom, but do your homework early and get it out of the way so you can study it at your leisure—not at the last, stressful minute.

By this stage of your job hunt, you should be completely familiar with the sources of company information in your library, online, or from social media, such as *Dun and Bradstreet's Million Dollar Directory, Standard & Poor's Register, Thomas Register,* and *Ward's Business Directory of U.S. Private Companies.* There are so many directories available that there is even a "Directory of Directories." Combine these formal information sources with what you find in the business press, from the Web, and what you have uncovered from your networking, and you will be able to develop a good picture of the company where you are interviewing.

Here are a few of the things you should know about your potential new employer before you go in for an interview:

➺ How it is owned: public or private.

➺ Size: number of employees, sales.

➺ Products and services.

➺ Financial health.

➺ Status in its industry.

➺ Legal problems, history, and status in the community.

➺ Family-friendly rating.

➺ Organizational culture.

➺ Key staff.

➺ Typical pay scales and benefit packages.

This Industry

No organization exists in a vacuum. If you are interviewing for a job in a not-for-profit (NFP) organization, you need to understand the effect that economic ups and downs have had on fundraising across the entire NFP world. If you are interviewing for a job in a pharmaceutical company, you need to have some background knowledge about orphan drugs, the FDA approval process, Medicare and Medicaid funding, and healthcare reform. Unless you are interviewing for one of the top jobs in the company, you don't have to be a bona fide expert on the entire industry, but you do need to be able to talk intelligently about the status of the industry, where it's headed, the current trends, the industry leaders, and so on.

Your reference librarian can help you uncover some of this information, but again I must stress that you must not leave this until the last minute. There are good sources of industry information out there, but not all of them are readily accessible. For example, finding the schedule of presentations from a recent industry trade show or convention, or tracking down a leading industry consultant to network with can take time.

And So On, and So On

We have progressed from having you prepared to talk about yourself to being prepared to talk about the job you're interviewing for, about the company, and about the industry. We could continue ad infinitum to the economy, the country, the world, the universe, and the cosmos beyond. The point here is that the more generally informed you are about the world around you, the more interesting you are as a person, and the more interesting you will be as a job candidate. You don't need to be a walking, talking encyclopedia, but reading the daily newspaper and listening to the evening news can be quite helpful in your overall interview preparation.

One of the ways for you to control the interview is not to see it as a big unknown. The unknown can translate into fear, fear can translate into stress, and stress can hurt your interview performance. Use Figure 5.1 on page 93 to help you think through your interview preparation. Your upcoming interview is *not* some big unknown; in fact, it is fairly predictable. Using this knowledge to thoroughly prepare will considerably reduce your fear, stress, and anxiety. You will have out-prepared your competition because every question you hear in your interview (even the ones that seem out of sequence or sound as if they're from left field) will fit somewhere into the interview plan you have meticulously constructed.

How to Answer a Question

The title of this section sounds almost humorous, sort of like "how to drink water" or "how to breathe air." I mean, after all, you've been answering questions all of your life, right? But as with every other part of the job-hunting and interviewing process, I want you better informed and better prepared than your competition. There is a big difference between a good answer and a great answer that makes them want to hire you today. There is a huge difference between the average job interview and a great job interview. Having thought through precisely how you want to field the interviewer's question is essential to this process.

1. Listen Actively to Each Question

Watch your interviewer's body language and facial expressions—especially his eyes. It is perfectly acceptable to ask the interviewer to make something clearer or to restate the question. Naturally, you don't want to do this after every question, but it is critical for you to know what the interviewer is trying to learn about you. Other forms of active listening that can help you here are paraphrasing or restating the question to confirm that you're both on the same wavelength.

2. Take a Second or Two to Frame Your Answer

You're not a gumball machine that the interviewer pops a quarter into and immediately out pops an answer. If you respond too quickly, it will sound as if you're over-programmed and not really thinking about your answers. (Of course, on the other side of the coin, if you respond too slowly, it may appear that you have drifted off to La-La Land.) You may have a great answer prepared and ready to go, but take a moment to understand what it is the interviewer is going for. We'll deal with stupid questions later, but sometimes ooking for the rationale behind a question can help you generate a stronger response.

3. Never Let Them Put Negative Words in Your Mouth

Using negative words makes you sound negative; using positive words makes you sound positive. This is a technique politicians have long known. Stay positive. Your last company wasn't the "hell-hole" as it was portrayed in the press; it was "full of challenges that helped me learn to deal productively with conflict." Your last boss wasn't a "mean S.O.B."; he was "demanding, but with a style very different from my own." This brings us to my next point.

4. Always Tell the Truth

Of course, it's the right thing to do morally, but also, the truth always makes the best answer because it looks and sounds like, well, the truth.

Quick quiz: what's the opposite of dishonesty? Most folks answer *honesty*, and most folks are wrong. A quick look at Figure 5.2 (Dr. Paul's Guide to Honesty and Survival) on the next page demonstrates that the polar opposite of dishonesty is brutal honesty—honesty without

Dr. Paul's Guide to Honesty and Survival

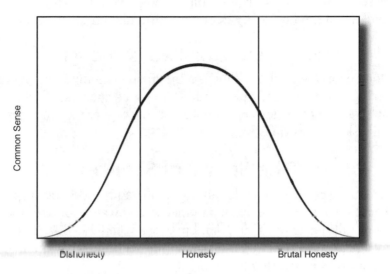

Dishonesty: "My boss was great."

Honesty: "My boss was tough but I can work with all types."

Brutal Honesty: "My boss was a tyrannical idiot."

Figure 5.2

common sense, honesty without compassion. People who have managed to stay married for a while usually have this figured out. Consider the question: "How was dinner?"

Which is the better answer?

a) "I wouldn't feed it to the dog!"

or,

b) "Interesting, but it can't compare to your famous chicken marsala."

Obviously, the answer is b. This may sound a little weasel-like, but you haven't really been dishonest; you've responded with sensitivity to the other person's feelings (not to mention with some common sense).

Staying positive while staying truthful will mean that you have to couch some of your answers carefully. Intelligent interviewers will know you are doing this, may try to explore the issue a little more, and will respect your savvy in staying positive. Remember, every potential employer sees himself as your potential ex-employer, and you will increase his comfort level with you by demonstrating tact and professionalism.

5. A Minute or Two Is Enough

Don't drone on and on. This is a big mistake many folks make when answering some of those open-ended questions such as, "Tell me about yourself." If the interviewer wants to get into something in great detail, she will ask another question.

The Sound of Silence

Try this experiment: while talking to a friend, suddenly stop talking, stay silent for four or five seconds (check your watch for accuracy), and then start talking again. Your friend may ask you if you dozed off or were having a heart attack or something. What this little experiment shows is how noticeable even a tiny bit of silence is.

When you are under some stress, this little bit of time may seem exaggerated. Thus, the few seconds it takes you to frame an answer or the time it takes an interviewer to ask the next question may seem overly long. Don't read too much into it, and don't worry about it—it's normal.

Psychotherapists have long understood the power of silence to get someone to open up. Some interviewers will use this technique on you. But you do not need to fill every second of airtime. Don't fidget or start adjusting your clothes.

If you have fully answered the last question, simply sit there quietly, take a couple of relaxing, deep breaths, and await the next question. If you have stumbled onto the dreaded idiot interviewer who thinks he can stress you out by staring at you, calmly return her gaze with a welcoming, anticipating look on your face.

Other interviewers may simply be struggling to find another good question to ask you. As we discussed earlier, many interviewers are not especially well-trained and try to take great care not to look foolish or say something stupid, or ask something that could be illegal. In fact, many interviewers hate interviewing and are more uncomfortable than the person they are interviewing. If you judge this to be the situation (after 15 seconds or so), mention that you have some questions that you would like to ask and see if this is an appropriate time to do so. If your interviewer is floundering, your offer will come as a godsend.

Ask and You Shall Receive

In the previous chapter we discussed the fact that you should look at the interview as a two-way street. Obviously, they are interviewing you, but, in reality, you are also interviewing them. You hope they will be offering you money for your work, but you are offering them weeks, months, and years of your life. What's more valuable in your book?

Because most good interviewers will ask you at some point if you have any questions, you need to have some good ones prepared. Even if the interviewer doesn't ask you if you have any questions, I want you to have some good ones prepared so that you can try to ask them. This happens most frequently toward the end of the interview.

The best questions you can ask in the interview can help you in two important ways. They transmit positive information about you to the Interviewer, and they get you data that will help you decide if this is where you want to work. Let's take them in turn.

Giving Data

You want your interviewer to assess you positively. You want her to know that you have done your homework and that you are very interested in the position and in the organization. Questions to help you accomplish these goals should be based on the research you have already done. Some examples are:

➳ "I read in your annual report that this company is rapidly expanding in Latin America. My Spanish is only fair to middling, but I'm interested in becoming more fluent. Does the training department offer courses in this area?" This question demonstrates three things: (1) you have done some homework on the company, (2) you have some tools that could be useful in a growth area of the company, and (3) you are interested in continuing to develop your skills.

➳ "I remember reading in the paper last year that St. Vitus Hospital merged with two other hospitals, one larger and one smaller. We went through something similar a few years back at Mercy General. I'm curious as to how the staff handled it—has the culture changed significantly?" This question demonstrates three things: (1) you are knowledgeable about the hospital and the industry, (2) you have some experience that is directly relevant to what this hospital may be going through, and (3) you are interested in the insight and observations of the interviewer.

Getting Data

If you are fortunate enough to get a job offer, what else do you need to know about the organization before you would accept it? Let this issue help you construct some other useful questions to ask in your interview. We will talk about money later, but beyond financial considerations, you want to be confident that you can succeed in the job, right? So use this golden opportunity to clarify as many issues as you can. Some examples are:

➻ "Can you show me an organizational chart? Because we're talking about a supervisory job in order management, I'm interested in how the group's relationship between sales and customer service is structured." Other questions you might ask: "Who are the managers of those groups? How do they interact? How do they get along?" These questions show that you are already identifying with the goals of your potential new department, that you are savvy enough to predict friction between certain groups, and that you will probably work proactively to sort out these types of issues early in your tenure.

➻ "Elroy, you've worked in this organization for a while. How would you describe the culture? What types of people seem to really succeed here?" This question demonstrates that you are interested in your interviewer's perceptions and opinions, it helps you get some inside information about the organization, and it may give you a shopping list of personal traits or characteristics that they are looking for in a new hire.

You will not get a huge amount of time to ask questions during your job interviews, so make each one count. Tool #8 in Chapter 10: Preparing Great Questions to Ask in Your Interview, gives you a systematic method for generating some intelligent and helpful questions. If you use this form to help you further prepare for your interview, you will be able to strengthen your candidacy for this job, gather data you might not be able to access in any other way, and possibly pick up subtle messages from the interviewer that he may not even know he is sending (for example, the number of other candidates that are in the loop and the degree of interest the company has in hiring you). Last but not least, you are giving the interviewer time to talk and because most people prefer talking to listening, this will ultimately work in your favor.

How Do You Get to Carnegie Hall?

A little girl walking down a New York City street stops a wise old man and asks, "Please sir, how do you get to Carnegie Hall?" He pauses, thinks, and says, "Practice, practice, practice."

There are only so many times in your career when you will be actively job hunting. A process you engage in only occasionally throughout the period of a couple of decades isn't something in which you will automatically develop a whole lot of proficiency. Add to this the relatively low number of bona fide interviews you will get during any active job search. What we end up with is a fairly rare, irregularly occurring task at which you want to be at peak-performance levels. This is a completely unrealistic expectation unless you get plenty of structured practice.

Some job hunters practice their interviewing skills during their first few interviews. Unfortunately, often these first few interviews are with the organizations they most want to work in. This results in job hunters using these critical skills at their lowest peak with their prime job targets. This is bad strategy and a bad tactic.

Before you ever walk into your first real job interview, I want you to have spent a minimum of four to six hours practicing your interviewing skills. Some job hunters have told me that this is excessive. Horse hockey! Your interviewing skills must be primed at the outset. The first position you interview for during this campaign could be the best one you encounter during the entire job hunt. This may seem excessively lucky to you, but luck is what happens to the well-prepared.

Solo Practice

The first part of practicing your interview skills should be done alone. Spend all the time you need on Tools #7 and #8 in the Toolkit (Frequently Asked Interview Questions and Preparing Great Questions to Ask in Your Interview). Compile a list of the questions that will be hardest for you to answer. With this list in front of you, ask yourself each question out loud. Yes, *each* question, and, yes, *out loud*. Then answer each question out loud. How does it sound? Where is it weak? How can it be improved? Does the answer demonstrate something about your personal characteristics, your knowledge, and your experience? Answer it again and again until it sounds solid, believable, and positive.

When you feel you have a good answer, note the number of the question in a spiral-bound notebook, and beside the question write down a few words or phrases that will bring your answer to mind. (As time permits, eventually work your way through all 107 questions.) Do not write out the entire text of the answer. You will be reviewing these notes later and you don't want to risk memorizing complete sentences that will make you sound like a recording. Working your way through the list will take a good amount of time, so start now. Many job hunters want to skip this step, however, I can't stress strongly enough that landing a job you can love for months and years of your life is darn well worth a few hours of work now.

Practice Interviews

For the second part of your interview practice program you will need a partner or two. This partner could be a spouse, a close friend, a counselor, a coach, or someone from your job-search support group. I suggest you use someone who is also currently job hunting because you can learn from each other's efforts.

Make a copy of Tool #9: Preparing for Your Practice Interviews. Fill in items 1 through 7 and then give it to your practice interviewer to add her questions to item 8. Now you have a script for your practice interview.

One way that you can quickly and dramatically improve your interviewing skills is to videotape your practice interviews and review them later with your interviewer. This, again, is something most job hunters resist. Unless you are often mistaken for Angelina Jolie or George Clooney, you are not going to be happy with the way you look on videotape. (I bet even Angie and George nitpick their appearance.) Get over it! What we're looking for, among other things, is how you come across to the interviewer, how you handle the questions, how you deal with the transition from answering questions to asking questions, and your overall personal presentation.

Today's video cameras are easy to use; if you don't own one, borrow one from a friend. Many of today's phones have this capacity, but connect it to your TV so you get the full benefit from the playback. Set the camera up on a bookcase or table so that it's focused solely on you, the job hunter. This isn't *60 Minutes*. We don't care how the interviewer comes across. Your interviewer should be someone who understands that although this may be a bit fun, it is important practice and serious business. (This is another good reason to recruit another job hunter for this job.) Once the camera is set and checked, start it up, re-enter the room as you would for an interview, and, with your partner using your script, role-play your interview for 50 to 60 minutes. If you make a mistake or make a misstatement, do not start over. Learning to come back from a bumble or a stumble is a valuable part of the process.

After your practice interview, do not review the tape alone; you will be far too critical of yourself. Do it with someone else, preferably your interview partner, who can tell you what it was like at the moment. Using Tool #10: Evaluating Your Practice Interview, evaluate yourself as if you were evaluating someone else. Be as dispassionate and objective as you can. The idea is neither to beat yourself up nor give yourself an automatic pat on the back. Your goal is to get feedback you can use to improve your next interview. Incorporate this information into your next practice interview and continue this process until your interviewing skills are honed to a razor's edge.

In Tool #10, you'll notice a few questions about uncovering objections and using a strong close. These are professional sales techniques refined by generations of successful salespeople. Understood and used properly, they will help you separate yourself from other merely good interviewers and distinguish yourself as a truly *great* job interviewer. They deserve some significant attention and focus of their own, so we'll devote Chapter 7 entirely to moving you from the short list to closing the deal and getting the job offer. But before we even think of closing the interview, an often overlooked but invaluable interviewing resource needs your attention—your job references. This is another step in which my knowledge and your time and energy in preparation are going to help you out-prepare your competition and advance you from a good job candidate to the great one that your prospective employer can't live without.

Chapter 6

Using the Ace up Your Sleeve

MAKE NO MISTAKE ABOUT IT; JOB HUNTING IS A COMPETITIVE ACTIVITY. If you have a tool at your disposal to improve the likelihood of a positive outcome, you would be foolish or lazy not to make the most use of it. The ace up your sleeve that I'm talking about here is your set of job references.

Your set of job references is an essential job-hunting tool. It is often given short shrift by job hunters. Some job hunters ask for a supervisor or two to be a reference and sit back, hoping they will say something positive if and when the time comes. Some wait until they are asked for references at the end of an interview before they give them much thought. Both approaches are dead wrong because:

1. Despite a person's best intentions, you never know what someone will say about you until you have at least discussed it with them.

2. The time to prepare your references is now—before you get out there interviewing—when you have the time and clarity

107

of mind to think who can best help you in this vital role and how best they can do it.

Why Bother?

The best reason for you to invest the time and energy to prepare a glowing set of references is because, most of the time, your references will be checked only if you are a bona fide finalist for the position. You will have worked your heart out to get to this point in the process, and there may well be only one more step between you and success. Sometimes references will be checked on a couple of finalists, but most often I hear employers say something such as, "If his references check out, let's make him an offer." This is where, as the old saying goes, there is often a slip between the cup and the lip.

Not all interviewers will ask you for your references. However, they will be requested more frequently as you move into ever more responsible positions in your career. I've seen estimates that references are not checked somewhere between 25 to 50 percent of the time. There are different reasons given for these low numbers. One is the perception that former employers are reluctant to say anything negative that could result in a lawsuit from a former employee. Another is that some former employers are wary of unwittingly omitting a piece of data that could get them sued by the new employer. One reason *I've* frequently seen is that some interviewers prefer to trust their own gut instincts more than they do data from an unknown party. Although all of this stuff is interesting, this should have no effect on you, the competent job hunter.

The fact that some interviewers will not be checking your references is just further proof that you are better educated about the hiring process than many of them are. The fact that *some* interviewers will check your references means that you must have them well prepared for *all* interviewers.

The Two Essentials of Timing

Do it now. *That's* when you have to start prepping your references. Even if you're not sure when your next job hunt will begin, start prepping your references *now*. You must think about your job references as the precious tools they are. You need to take them out and inspect them every once in a while just to make sure they're in good shape for when you're going to need them next. If they need polishing and updating, now is the time to do it. And if you're currently in the job hunt, you don't have a minute to lose.

You need to start prepping your references now, ahead of time, before you're asked to provide them. Unless you are a *Jeopardy!* champion, you're probably not at your best when trying desperately to retrieve important facts from your brain while under pressure. Adequately preparing your job references takes time, and once you're asked for them, the clock is ticking. You need time to think of who you want as references. You need to think about how you're going to ask them. You may need time to track them down if some are from one or two jobs ago. Then you need time to contact them. You need time for them to call or e-mail you back. And you need time to meet with them, preferably face to face. Oh, and multiply this amount of time by the number of references you need to prepare. I suggest four as a minimum. Given this reality, don't start now—start yesterday.

There is a second very important reason for you to start prepping your references early in the job hunt. Unless you are seriously masochistic, you will be using references who have positive things to say about you. Because these people already think highly of you (and you'll soon be reminding them of just *how* highly), why not ask for their assistance early in your job hunt? These people are a unique part of your contact network. Tap their expertise the way you would any network contact. Ask them what sources of published openings they know of. What online resources or career Websites are they aware of? Do they know of or have access to an especially great resource library? Do they have any human resources contacts, or can they personally refer you to an employment recruiter? Do they have any potential job leads or any other creative job-hunting resources for you? Will they refer you to others to help you expand your network? And, of course, are they willing to be contacted as a reference for you?

Should all professional and conscientious hiring managers check references? Absolutely. Should all professional and conscientious job candidates have a well-prepared set of job references? Absolutely. If your interviewer doesn't ask for your references, should you offer them? Absolutely *not*. Take a quick look back at Figure 3.1 on page 66. This is to remind you that checking references is one more step between you and the job offer. Just because you have a great set of references all prepared and ready to go does *not* mean you need to use them. The answer to the question, "When do I give my references?" is: *only after there is a strong mutual desire to move forward and only when you are asked for them.*

If you are not going to actively pursue the position in question, do not offer your references. Why would you bother these people who are willing to go out of their way to help you if you don't really need their help? Your references are valuable resources, so keep them in reserve for when you actually need them. To the latter point, if an organization wants to hire you without running you (and your references) through another step in this long and hard process, so be it. For goodness' sake, don't remind them that there's another potential hurdle for you to jump; that's their problem, not yours.

Pick Your References Wisely

Who you should use for references depends, to some degree, on what type of job you're hunting for. The most frequently requested job reference is your most recent boss. If you are currently employed and your boss doesn't know you're job hunting, this presents a bit of a problem. My advice in this situation is to offer your previous boss. If the interviewer still wants to talk to your current boss, remember that Dr. Paul has advised you that you are under no obligation to commit career suicide. There are ways around this, however.

You may belong to that fortunate minority who has a boss who wants you to succeed in your career and realizes that, sometimes, for that to happen, people have to move on. If you can trust your boss not to penalize you for job hunting, you know it right at the moment you will read this. You are indeed a fortunate person. Have a heart-to-heart talk with your boss and prepare him or her as you would any other reference. If you are at all uncertain about it, don't risk blowing your cover. Tell your interviewer that you will be happy to provide all of your references, including one from your current boss, with the understanding that references from your current organization will be checked *only after* you have a written offer in hand, an agreed-upon start date, and the opportunity to give your current employer adequate notice of your resignation. If your potential new employer is not willing to treat you professionally and with respect, and does not value your desire to make a career transition in a civil and dignified manner by not leaving your employer in a lurch, well, what does that tell you? Maybe this isn't such a great place to work after all. After all the work you put in to find this employer, it's a damn shame to discover this, but it's better to know it earlier than later.

You should have two (and preferably three) former bosses prepared to use as references. If you have supervised or managed other people, you should also have a couple of key former subordinates on your reference list. If you have or have had responsibilities for managing relationships outside of your employing organization (for example, vendors, suppliers, contractors, consultants, and volunteers), you should have a few of them prepared, as well. Do not use people such as your clergyperson, your accountant, your best friend, or your neighbor. These are personal references and are more appropriate for a credit card, rental, or mortgage application.

Preparing Your References

You have now decided who you should be using for references: articulate, positive, helpful people who can speak cogently about your knowledge, experience, work habits, and interpersonal skills. Once you have compiled your list of potential references, start calling them.

The purpose of this call is to renew your acquaintance (chitchat about people you know in common, update family matters, and so on), bring them up to date on your job hunt, and ask for a meeting to discuss your reference. Period. The purpose of the call is *not* to prepare your reference. Can you do this by phone? Sure, if meeting personally is out of the question. But meeting in person is the *best* way of securing the most positive reference possible. Your job is to have great—not merely good—references, and the way to do this is to out-prepare your competition. Of course, if this person is on the other side of the country or abroad, it will not be possible. But don't take the lazy way out if your references are local.

When you meet for coffee, breakfast, or lunch, take a copy of the Job Reference Data Form (Tool #12 in the Chapter 10 Toolkit) with you. Ask if she can offer you some ideas or tips about your job search and let her advise you. (Everybody likes to be asked for advice.) Then, pop the question, "So, Linda, would you be willing to serve as a reference for me?" or something like that. But ask the question directly. If she has reservations, it's better for you to know it now.

Start filling out the form as you are talking and make sure to find out how and where they prefer to be contacted—at home, at work, cell phone, private line, e-mail, and so on. Refresh your reference's memory as to how long you've known each other and in what roles and in what organizations. On pages 110–111 you will find a list of many of the reference questions I have heard during the last 30 years. Pick the ones you feel are most appropriate to the position you are looking for and discus them with your reference. The reason for doing this is to expand the reference data beyond the generic "he's great" or "she's terrific" comments that won't do you much good. You want to help your reference remember specifics: all the great things you did together; all the successes you had; how you dealt with setbacks; and, yes, what a great person you are. This means, of course, that you will have already spent some time resurrecting these memories yourself. Be sure to discuss your strengths and weaknesses and be ready to suggest some with which you are comfortable.

Another reference question that's almost guaranteed to be asked is why you left the job your reference is discussing. Ask who else he might offer as a reference if the interviewer asks for someone else to talk to. To help prevent this process from going too far afield, it's a savvy idea to have two people prepared to suggest each other. Continue to make notes during this conversation so that you can recall later who will be saying what. When your meeting is over, remember to thank your reference and indicate that you will do your best to give him a heads-up prior to being contacted. This is an obvious courtesy, but it also gives you the chance to help fine-tune the reference with your input about the interviewer, the company, and the specific job in question.

When you go home or get back to the office, immediately send a note thanking your reference for her advice, support, and willingness to serve as a reference. Include a copy of your updated resume and a copy of the Job Reference Data Form that you just completed. This gives your reference plenty of data to draw upon when called, and it helps reinforce the message that you are an appreciative, thoughtful, and well-organized professional. Now you can add this person's name and contact information to your reference list. (See Tool #13: Sample Job References Listing Sheet in the Chapter 10 Toolkit.)

Typical Reference Questions

→ How long have you known him and in what roles?

→ What was her salary?

→ How would you describe his personality?

→ What are her strengths and weaknesses? Can you give me a situation where you observed them?

→ What was the quality of his work?

➤ What are her work habits?

➤ Why did he leave the company?

➤ Would you hire her back if you could?

➤ Did he require a lot of supervision? How independent is he?

➤ How much responsibility did she have?

➤ Do you know if he has ever been fired?

➤ What would her peers and subordinates tell me about her?

➤ Can you give me an example of how he learned from an error he made?

➤ How does she handle conflict?

➤ What frustrates him?

➤ How does she handle pressure and deadlines?

➤ What could he have done to improve his performance?

➤ Do you think this job fits in with her long-range career plans? Why or not?

➤ What would be the ideal role for him?

➤ What motivates her?

➤ What turns him off?

➤ Given the scope of this job, what kind of a fit do you see here?

➤ Can you think of anything else that would help me get a more well-rounded picture of him?

➤ Who else would be a good person for me to talk to about her?

How to Avoid Reference Glitches

As with everything else in job hunting, there are a few potential glitches that you might run into in the reference process. Not to worry, there are ways you can deal with all of them. The important thing is not to panic—stay cool—and work your way around them.

The "No-Reference" Policy

Some organizations have a "no-reference" policy. They may only provide dates of employment, job title, and salary. If you run into this, you can ask your reference if he would be willing to give you a *personal* reference. (If he won't, he won't. There's nothing else you can do. Move on to someone else.) However, because you are asking people who already think highly of you to help, most of them will. Be sure to double-check where and how they prefer to be contacted.

It is perfectly appropriate to inform your interviewer that this particular employer has a "no-reference" policy and that you have asked for a personal reference. Most hiring managers have run into this before and know how to tread gently in this area, because if they come on too strong they will get little or no additional information.

The Negative Reference

There are two types of negative references. One is the back-stabbin' SOB who you prepared, who indicated that he would say great things about you and then rips you up behind your back. If you have taken the time to prepare your references, this probably won't happen, because you can usually see in someone's eyes if they are being genuine with you. This goes to the point that even though you prepared a reference, you still may not want to use him or her. It is up to you to determine if the person, will in fact be a good reference for you. But on a rare occasion, you might get sandbagged. You'll only find out about this if the interviewer shares it with you. Obviously, you'll never offer this person as a reference again, but right now you need a response.

I suggest that you express your honest surprise and take the high road. You might say something such as, "I hope the fact that this person would say great things to my face and then turn around and say negative things behind my back says more about him than me. In any event, I would be pleased to have you speak with someone else who can comment on my performance in that job and see how they viewed me." And then offer another reference. (This is another reason why you can never have too many references prepared.) This is damage control, but it's the best you can do. Forget about this loser. Life and karma have many ways to balance the scales of justice. Remember, time not only heals all wounds, it also wounds all heels.

The other negative reference is someone (such as a former boss) who may not be one of your strongest supporters, whose name you obviously did not supply, but who is well-known and who may be called regardless of whether you supplied his name or not. Perhaps he even fired you. Even if this is the case, I still want you to make an effort to prepare him as a reference. Time may have softened his opinion of you. He may recognize the difficult position that you were in at the time. At the very least, ask him to give a balanced picture of your contributions if he is contacted. Obviously, don't offer this person as a reference in the first place if you can help it; if you are forced to, always pair him with another reference who is familiar with whatever the situation was and who will give it a more positive perspective.

Missing in Action

"I can't find my old boss." "I can't remember that VP's name." "That job was years ago; who would be interested now?" "That company has been bought and sold twice since I was there. Nobody's left who would remember me." I hear this stuff a lot. I try to be supportive, but I really just want to say, "You should have never misplaced your references in the first place. You've only made more work for yourself. Now get back to work and go find them."

These are *your* references. You've worked long and hard for them. You've earned them. They are an invaluable interviewing resource. I don't have time now to beat you up about not having maintained them the way you were supposed to. You have to get going as soon as possible and track them down. Use your other contacts, former colleagues, phone books, old Rolodex, professional associations, trade groups, alumni associations, and, of course, the Web and your social networking sites. Once you have rebuilt your reference list, never let it get out of date again. Think of excuses (Christmas, birthdays, Groundhog Day) to stay in touch. You will need your job references for as long as you are in the working world, so give them the time and energy they deserve.

Closing the Loop

You've thoroughly prepared a solid reference list, you've offered it to the interviewer (but only when requested), you've alerted your references as to who will be calling, and you've told them a little about why you are perfect for the job. The sum total of your interviewing and job references may get you the job offer you want. Or the job opening may be put on hold, or they might promote from within, or they may hire someone else from the outside, or they may reopen the search. Or, or, or. Regardless of what happens, at this point get another note out to your references thanking them for taking the time to speak with the interviewer on your behalf. Not only is this common courtesy, but it also keeps your support team involved, informed, and motivated to keep helping you.

Three Last Things

I have three final pieces of advice for you regarding your job references.

Letters of Recommendation

In the era before phone, fax, and e-mail, letters of recommendation were commonly used. This is not the case today. In our increasingly litigious society, nobody wants to put anything negative down on paper about someone else, so any letters are uniformly positive and usually dismissed as fluff. You will still see job advertisements in education and some scientific journals requesting them, and first-time job hunters still use them. But for anything other than an entry-level job, your interviewer will want to speak to some live human beings.

As with most rules, there are exceptions. If one of your references will be incommunicado during a significant part of your job hunt (on the international space station or paddling up the Congo in a dugout canoe, for example), then you may want to secure a letter of recommendation. But, otherwise, don't bother.

Security Clearances

If you are being interviewed for a sensitive government job, for a defense contractor, or for a position in homeland security, you will probably be screened for security clearance. Whereas your job references focus on your job performance, a security clearance investigation includes a lot of other stuff, such as taking your fingerprints, checking your legal/court records, verifying all your old addresses and your foreign travel, talking to current and former neighbors, and, generally, compiling a complete file on where you've been and what you've done for your whole life.

If this is the sort of job you want, you'll need to come to terms with this process. I find the idea of scary people with big guns asking the neighbors all about me kind of cool; it creates just the mystique I'm going for. But if you want to keep a low profile with the government (as if they don't know everything already), positions in these fields may not be for you.

Credit Checks

It seems as if we're getting pretty far afield from job references, but we're not. Many organizations hiring a senior executive will conduct a credit check along with checking job references to get a handle on how this person manages his or her own financial affairs. In the United States you can check your credit rating with the major credit rating agencies for free once a year. Even if this is not the case where you live, fiscal prudence in the era of identity theft suggests that you should do so anyway.

➤➤ ➤➤ ➤➤

I know this chapter has outlined a more comprehensive reference preparation regimen than you are probably used to. I know it involves a lot of work. I also know it will help you stand head and shoulders above your competition. Make no mistake about it: there are other job hunters out there who are competing with you for the job you want, and their references are tuned up tighter than violin strings. My question to you is this: do you want this job badly enough to do what it takes to win it? If you do, then you are well on your way—with a pocketful of great references—to a job you can love.

The issue of job references will only arise after a level of interest is expressed, usually toward the end of the interview. It's important not to let the interview end on this tentative "let's wait and see what the references have to say" note. Successful salespeople—those who make a fabulous living by selling goods or services to other people—know that how a meeting, a sales call, or a job interview concludes has a powerful effect on the ultimate result. In Chapter 7 you will learn how the techniques of successful salespeople can help you bring your job hunt to a great conclusion.

Chapter 7

Making the Job Offer Happen

WAITING AND HOPING ARE *NOT* THE JOB HUNTING SKILLS THAT I WANT YOU TO IMPROVE. I'm betting that you're already pretty good in those departments. The professional job search requires many skills: self-assessment skills, research skills, organizational skills, telephone skills, administrative skills, marketing skills, communication skills, follow-up skills, and personal presentation skills. I've met many good job hunters who need improvement in each of these areas. But most of them, like you, are already pretty good at waiting and hoping for something good to happen. To get them from being good job hunters to being great job hunters, I often have to get them to back off of their hoping and waiting skills and improve at all the others in order to get some real forward momentum going.

I mentioned in an earlier chapter that if you find yourself job hunting, you need to realize that you are now in a sales position. However, most people in the world of work are *not* skilled salespeople. Heck, even some people employed as salespeople aren't skilled salespeople. The statistical likelihood is that you are not a salesperson. This reality often causes job hunters to feel a surge of panic. Don't worry about this; salespeople are created, not born. Plus, you probably don't have any bad sales habits to unlearn. If you are a salesperson, I don't need to remind you that some of your colleagues are not very good at it. (This is one of the reasons that salespeople are sometimes held in such low regard.) Even if you are in the top one percent of super salespeople, this chapter will help you incorporate your superior sales skills into great job interviews that will generate more job offers. In this chapter I will explain how the ordinary job hunter can use the secrets of the super salesperson to convert a higher percentage of those hard-won job interviews into bona fide job offers. You can do this, so pay attention.

Sales Myths

There are many misconceptions about professional selling. One is that the sale is a contest of wills—one in which the salesperson keeps talking and talking so that she wears down a resistant buyer until, ultimately, they both collapse in an exhausted heap over a completed deal. Nothing could be further from the truth. Any professional sale of goods or services should be a meeting of the minds, a meeting in which the salesperson learns the needs and desires of the buyer and where the buyer learns how the product or service the seller is offering can help meet her needs and desires. If the salesperson is not actively listening for the potential buyer's needs, the sale will not happen. If the salesperson is preaching ("my product is great") rather than teaching ("here's *why* my product is great"), the sale will not happen. These two points reinforce why an effective job interview must be an exchange of ideas, not a one-way infomercial.

Another sales myth is that there is only one successful sales personality. The stereotypical image of the successful salesperson is that of a sharply dressed, fast-talking extrovert. Although some personality types do have an easier time learning professional sales techniques, many low-key, informal introverts make excellent salespeople. (Warren Buffet, investor extraordinaire, and Bill Gates, who built the biggest software company in the world, come to mind.) Regardless of what type of personality you have, you can learn and easily use super sales techniques to your enormous advantage.

The last sales myth I'll touch on here is that some things sell themselves. What hooey. Every product or service must be fully and engagingly described to the potential buyer in a way that demonstrates how it meets the buyer's needs and desires. You couldn't sell chocolate-covered bars of gold bullion for 10¢ a pound unless you knew how to fit their desirable characteristics to the needs and desires of the customer, and then (drum roll, please) help your buyer overcome whatever objections he may have, logical or illogical, so that you can close the deal.

What Is a "Close"?

In the terms of professional sales training, the "close" is when you strive to uncover any objections or reservations your potential customer has, and you help your potential customer communicate the decision she has made during your presentation. Notice I said *help* your potential customer, not intimidate, dominate, or bludgeon. An intelligent potential buyer (and you must assume this of your interviewer) will resist any effort by you to manipulate or overwhelm him even *if* he has already made a potential buying decision in your favor. No one likes being manipulated or overwhelmed.

There are those few occasions when some buyers can be bullied or mesmerized into putting their name on the dotted line or saying yes, but getting them to follow through (that is, putting through the purchase order or taking delivery) will be next to impossible. They were probably just agreeing with you to get you out of their office.

A close is successful if the buyer immediately responds and says, "Yes, I love what you're selling; when can it be delivered?" Interestingly, the close is also successful if it succeeds in uncovering an objection that the buyer has to the sale. It is only by discovering potential objections that the salesperson can tailor her presentation to more fully explain how her product or service can meet the needs and desires of the potential buyer. If those objections exist but remain hidden, undiscovered, or unspoken, they cannot be overturned; the sale will not happen, and, even worse, the salesperson will never know why.

You Mean I *Want* Objections?

In a word, yes. Your job interview is a sales call in which you communicate your knowledge, skills, experience, and personal qualities in an effort to demonstrate that you meet and, you hope, even exceed the needs and desires of the potential buyer. Through your pre-interview research and by asking insightful interview questions, you have uncovered these needs (the job specifications). Via your interview answers, you have succinctly but completely presented the reasons why you can do the job in question. Now you need to *help your potential customer express the decision he has made during your presentation*.

The Trial Close

The trial close involves asking a question to get a feeling for how ready your buyer is to make a decision. After you have answered a question about some aspect of your background that closely relates to the job you're interviewing for, an effective trial close might be, "Dr. Waggle, I'm really glad you asked me about my dog training experience. When I was thinking about this interview, I was hoping you'd agree that such experience would be a great asset to someone working in your animal clinic." Notice this is one of those "non-question questions." You're not forcing her to respond, but if she does, there are three potential outcomes:

1. Dr. Waggle agrees with you and tells you that she is ready to hire you. This is the best news. You can stop selling and start working out the details.

2. Dr. Waggle agrees with you and asks another question. This is also good news in that she has bought one of your selling points and is now moving on to discover more.

3. Dr. Waggle disagrees with you. But how you handle this disagreement—this objection—can still provide you with a selling opportunity.

Let's look at another example of a trial close. It's nearing the end of your interview. You've been asked a lot of questions, and you've asked a couple of good ones yourself. Try something like this: "Mr. Adler, I realize our time is starting to get short. I've really enjoyed learning more about AdVentures and I think I could be very successful here. [*Pause a moment here to look for some nonverbal feedback.*] What questions or issues have I left unanswered?"

Notice a few things that are built into this trial close. You have shown appropriate courtesy, which is always a good idea. (I don't call it "common courtesy," because these days it's not so common.) You have expressed strong interest in the job and have given your positive evaluation of the fit between your background and the needs of the job. You're not blaming Mr. Adler for not having asked enough questions; you're accepting that *you* might have left something unsaid. You have left Mr. Adler with an opportunity to endorse your candidacy and suggest a positive next step. And most importantly, if Mr. Adler has a reservation about your candidacy, you have offered him the opportunity to get it out in the open so that you can address it or, even better, overturn it.

Very few job hunters can think up great trial closes on the spur of the moment such as the ones presented here. This is why Tools #10, #11, and #14 in the Toolkit all have sections to help you prepare, practice, and evaluate how you can close your interviews on the strongest note possible.

When Do You Use a Trial Close?

There are three answers to this question. The trial close used in the interview with Dr. Waggle at the Springfield Animal Clinic example demonstrates an old sales axiom that you can remember with the letters A-B-C, which stands for *Always Be Closing*. In job interviewing, this works only after some level of mutual interest is established. If you come on too strong, too early, it won't work. But after you're well into the interview and if you have a strong feeling that it's going well, you might slip in one of those "non-question questions" and see how you're really doing.

The traditional time to try a trial close in the job interview is demonstrated in the AdVentures example. Working it in near the end of the interview has a more natural feel to it, but it comes with a risk. Your interviewer may indicate more than one possible objection. This is not necessarily a deal-breaker, but if you have only another five or 10 minutes left in the interview, you may not have time to address them all. This is why it's usually a good strategy to try to slip in a subtle trial close when you estimate that you have at least 25 percent of your interview time remaining.

In my consulting practice I've had the opportunity to work with a number of highly successful salespeople. More than a few have told me that there is no single best time to try to close a sale. What they suggest is to always be on the lookout for a buying signal. Whenever they see or hear a buying signal, they will use a trial close to solidify the progress they've made up to that point and to see if the potential buyer has made up his or her mind.

Buying Signals

Interviewers transmit two kinds of buying signals: overt and covert. A great job interviewer can pick up on both and seize the opportunity for a trial close. The *overt* buying signals are the ones we love to hear and are easy to pick up on. They include:

➳ "You sound like our kind of person."

➳ "That specific experience or skill would be quite useful to us."

➳ "What kind of notice would you have to give your current employer?"

➳ "I think you'll fit right in."

➳ "When can you start?"

It's important to stay focused and remember that you still have to close the interview on the strongest possible note. Despite the very positive impression these buying signals may give you, nobody has yet said, "You're hired!"

Covert buying signals from the interviewer are a lot subtler and may only consist of well-prepared questions designed to dig below the surface of your candidacy. This is good news because it shows a growing level of interest in you. After hearing a few of these signals, you should work in a trial close. Some samples of *covert* buying signals are:

➳ "That's a good approach. How do you think it would work here?"

➳ "I love that story. That stuff happens here all the time."

➳ "That makes sense on the supplier side, but tell me how it would work on the user side."

➳ "How would you recommend that we restructure that department?"

➳ "Your approach makes sense to me."

Here's How to Put Them Together

You've picked up on a buying signal or two, you've tried a trial close, and (surprise, surprise!) you've uncovered an objection. Remember, this is a good thing. Your interviewer had an objection and you succeeded in uncovering it. That was your goal. Don't get defensive, because if you do, you won't be able to truly understand the point your interviewer is trying to make. And if you don't fully understand her point, you won't be able to deal with it effectively.

What is helpful to understand here is how the job specification or description was compiled in the first place. Human resources professionals tell me that very few job descriptions are real works of art. Although some may be accurate descriptions of the job to be filled, others may just be a list of the duties of the person who last had the job. It may be a supervisor's wish list describing a virtual super-person, or it may be a minimal, bare-bones list suitable for a job posting. It's going to be darn hard to get a candidate that is an exact fit to a job specification that, itself, is far from precise. Some candidates will be stronger in one area than another. Some candidates will bring attractive and much-needed skills that don't even appear in the job description. In short, one of the reasons you are not the perfect job candidate for a particular job is because there probably are no perfect job candidates for any particular job.

Another important point to remember is that the purpose of this interview is to get a job offer, not to win you a debating trophy. An objection is a detour, not a roadblock. You don't need to change the interviewer's mind on every single point any more than you need to fix every pothole you find in the road. The interviewer is a human being whose observations are as worthy of respect as yours are. Treating his objection respectfully communicates your professionalism and your objectivity.

The objection you've uncovered doesn't necessarily mean that you won't get the job. In fact, how you handle the objection may well account for your landing the job.

To Overturn or Address an Objection

Let's go back to the AdVentures example. In that trial close you told Mr. Adler that having learned more about his organization, you thought you could succeed in it. Though hoping for some positive feedback, you wisely left the door open for any additional issues or questions. Let's say Mr. Adler raises the following potential objection.

"I've enjoyed our meeting, too. You've got a great background, but AdVentures is a small organization. What I'm concerned about is that all of your experience is with large companies." Okay, this is a fair assessment, and it's one that you should have seen coming as you prepared for this interview. Also, this is another strong reason to prepare separately for each and every interview. That way, you have the time to analyze your strengths and weaknesses relative to each position you're interviewing for, and you don't rely on your generic preparation.

Remember, you're here for a job, not a debate. (Plus, if you have my kind of luck, Mr. Adler is the former captain of the college debate team.) You don't necessarily have to change Mr. Adler's mind. What you have to do is give his observation its due respect and decide if you can overturn it, or if the best you can do is address it. Unless there's some big hole in your resume (that you now must explain), we'll say Mr. Adler's observation is correct. This means you can't overturn his objection, but you can address it. Here's how.

Take a moment and think through the interviewer's objection and look at it from his perspective. What concerns would you have if you were hiring a big-company person for a job in a small company? With this in mind, a good possible response could be something like this: "I see your point, Mr. Adler. But in my last job, the leasing group I supervised operated more like an independent business unit. I helped our team develop a real entrepreneurial attitude, and because we had to live off of our own revenues, we all had to wear different hats. I really enjoyed that. In fact, it was that experience that convinced me I could be a lot more successful in an organization like yours."

Okay, maybe you didn't exactly have this kind of experience. What types of entrepreneurial situations *have* you been in? What convinced you that you should work in one now? You must have some good reason for wanting to go from a big company to a small company. When you prepare for these potential objections, remember Figure 5.2, Dr. Paul's Guide to Honesty and Survival. Don't go saying something brutally honest, such as, "If I had to fill out another requisition form in triplicate for a box of stupid paper clips, I would have gone postal." Show due respect, think the objection through objectively, respond to overturn or address it, and always wrap up by mentioning one of your strong points.

Let's look at another example so I can throw in another wrinkle. Your trial close for the Springfield Animal Clinic job suggested that one element of your background (having dog training experience) would be a strong selling point. Let's say that your trial close has reminded Dr. Waggle of an item from her wish list that suddenly has arisen out of nowhere as an objection to your candidacy. She says, "Yes, dog training experience would be helpful, but we deal with all kinds of animals here, and I was really hoping to hire someone who was working her way through veterinary school." Even though this element may never have come up before, don't panic. Think it through. What is behind this objection? It's not as easy to figure out as the distinction between a large company and a small company. Frankly, it's not clear what the heck she's driving at.

When this is the case, you need to ask a clarifying question such as, "I wasn't aware you were looking for a vet student. I didn't catch that in the position description. What do you hope someone like that would bring to the technician position?" She may say they would be smart, or they would have an opportunity to see in practice what was being taught in school, or that *she* worked as a vet tech, while she was in school, or that she *wished* she had been a vet tech or who knows what else. The important thing is that you now have found out what's behind the objection. The rest of the plan stays the same. Offer due respect: "I can see how that would be helpful." Then think it through and respond to overcome or address it. "I'm hoping to take some vet tech courses myself after I get a handle on my new work schedule." And finally, wrap up on a strong point: "But what I hope you consider is that what I'm looking for is a vet tech job—not a stepping stone to something else. Plus, I don't have exams and hospital rotations to worry about, so overtime and the occasional weekend won't be a problem."

When you uncover an objection, *the interviewer is not objecting to you as a person*. He is giving voice to his fears, his concerns about your potential job performance, or maybe even his biases or stereotypes. These things do exist, and it is your job to get them out in the open so they can be dealt with. Otherwise, they will work against you after the interview when you have no opportunity to respond. If you can overcome the interviewer's fears, overturn his biases, and address his concerns, you will discover for yourself that uncovering and handling objections provides you with strong selling opportunities that the other candidates may never get.

Prepare for Obstacles

Let's look at some obstacles to your strong close.

The Unprepared

You will find that some interviewers are woefully unprepared for you. At first you may think this is good news, but it's really not. You *want* the interviewer to have a handle on what she is actually looking for so you can target your responses accordingly. There are some dim-witted interviewers out there (who obviously don't have enough to do) that keep interviewing a string of folks until it occurs to them that this or that person can probably do the job in question.

Using a trial close to uncover potential objections with these folks is next to impossible, because they don't have a clear picture of what they are looking for. Thus, it is impossible for them to see where you meet their needs and where you don't. Sadly, this is not the only type of resistance you will encounter.

The Control Freak

Some untrained interviewers are afraid the interview will get away from them. They will not let you get a question or a trial close in to save your life. You can recognize this person because he will have an interview outline, usually with 25 or so questions. The plan is that your answers, at approximately two minutes apiece, will take about 50 minutes, and he will try to leave about 10 minutes at the end to answer "any questions you may have."

This is not as bad as it seems. At least he knows what he wants to learn about you. Sometimes, after a comfortable rapport is established (that is, he feels comfortable and in control), you can work in a question. Make your first one something specific you want to learn about the potential assignment or the organization. Then let him ask a few more questions, putting him firmly back in the driver's seat. Only then do you try a trial close.

The Screening Interviewer

Your first interview may be conducted over the phone or in person with a human resources person, an employment agency, or someone else not from the department you're hoping to join. These people have been assigned to screen applicants to determine a preliminary list of potential candidates. Typically, they are not the hiring manager for whom you hope to work.

They don't have the appropriate position or the power to hire you, but they will determine whether you continue in the hiring process. So even with screening interviews, it is wise to use a trial close to ensure that there are no objections to your candidacy at this point.

You

These professional sales techniques will not work if you take criticism, negative feedback, or objections personally. It helps to remember that you are essentially an unknown quantity to these strangers who are interviewing you. If they have a potential objection to your candidacy, then *you* have done an incomplete job of telling them all the wonderful things you can do for them. Their objections have given you a golden opportunity for which you should be thankful.

These professional sales techniques will not work if you don't practice them. Practice includes preparing for potential objections, preparing clarifying questions, and thinking through how to overcome or address each one of them for every interview you go to. Reading about them isn't enough; thinking about them isn't enough. You need practice so you won't sound artificial.

These professional sales techniques will not work if you don't believe they will work. You won't hurt my feelings if you feel this way, but do yourself a favor and talk to a couple of *successful* professional salespeople. Ask them if it's true that objections pave the road to sales. Ask them if the best closers are the best sellers. Ask them if they use these skills (they probably do), and if they share their prized closing technique with others (they probably don't). Ask them if they think you can learn to use these skills (with practice) in your successful job interviews—they probably do!

You Want It? Ask for It!

Now that you know what a trial close is, how to uncover potential objections, and how to address or overturn them, it's time for the actual close. In professional sales training it's called *asking the big question*—asking for the sale. Job interviewing isn't exactly like the sales of professional services or products; in traditional sales, you would ask for the sale by saying something such as, "So, Ms. Ethier, we've talked about features, and we've talked about your budget and delivery needs, both of which we can meet. Can we sign an agreement for this system this afternoon?" You have reminded the buyer of what you have discussed and how you have met her objections, and you have asked for the sale.

Now the buyer has to answer yes or give you another objection, which you'll do your best to handle. Then you try again to close the sale. Maybe another objection arises. Again, you do your best to overturn or address it and back in for the close you go. This might seem almost self-abusive, but some sales trainers suggest that five, six, or even seven attempts to close a sale may be needed before a salesperson will get a firm yes or no.

Any seasoned salesperson will tell you that this is the hardest part of the sales process. A lot of salespeople go on and on about what they are selling, but never manage to get to the part where they ask the big question. This is why you will often hear sales managers say that there are many salespeople out there, but few good closers. With my coaching you can be both.

Because very few hiring decisions are made on the spot at the end of the interview, it wouldn't work very well for you to say something along the lines of, "Aren't I great? Can I start tomorrow?" You need to be subtler. But even being appropriately subtle will still bring the job offer closer to you than it will to the job candidate who lets the interview end with a whimper ("Thank you. I hope to hear from you, Mr. Burns") rather than with a good, strong close.

Tell 'em You Want It

One of the strongest possible ways to close an interview is to tell the interviewer that you want the job. Hey, that's the reason you're in there for the interview, right? Some folks have debated me on this point. They say they are there to see if there is a good fit, to see if the pay is fair, to see if there is growth opportunity. There are names for these people— back-up job candidates and runners-up. While they are embarked on this intellectual voyage of discovery, some other job candidate is going to get in there, make a strong presentation, uncover and deal with potential objections, focus on closing the deal, and get the job offer. Then that person will be the one assessing the fit, the compensation, and the growth opportunity. In other words, you can't decide whether or not you'll join the organization until you get the job offer, and that—the offer—is the objective of the interview.

Let's look at a couple of examples of how you might do this. Going back to the Springfield Animal Clinic case, you could use something like the following: "Dr. Waggle, this is exactly the type of job I'm looking for. I have a background working with animals and I'm good with them. I have a strong interest in learning more about the field, and I have the work habits that make me a good team player and a good employee. When you make your decision, I hope you decide to hire me." Whew, how could she resist? She might say she has some more people to interview (often true), that she will not be making her decision until next week, or something else. At that point, stay upbeat, thank her for her time, and reiterate that you look forward to hearing something positive.

For another approach that directly takes into account a possible objection, let's go back to the AdVentures example. (Remember that Mr. Adler had a concern about your lack of small-company experience.) A good close might go something like this: "Thanks for having me in today, Mr. Adler. I really enjoyed it. AdVentures is just the type of organization I'm looking for because here I can combine my solid corporate experience with my natural entrepreneurial drive. If you make the decision to hire me, and I hope you do, you won't be disappointed." If the potential objection seems central to the job, there is no sense trying to dodge it. Try to put a positive spin on it, as in this example, by positioning it as bringing solid business skills to a small, fast-moving company. And then finish up by hitting the strong point of your small-company, entrepreneurial attitude.

The Power of Desire

Do you remember junior high or middle school when a friend told you someone had a crush on you? Regardless of whether or not you had any interest in that person, you now viewed that person differently (more positively). You might not have been attracted to him or her, but you couldn't deny his or her good judgment and taste, right? In some cases, this reappraisal could lead to including this person in your social circle, to a friendship, or even to a relationship. This is evidence of the impact of being desired, and there are few things as powerful as desire.

Let's move forward to a time in your adult life when you were dating. You have been with someone a while and he says, "I love you." Regardless of whether or not you are looking or hoping for a long-term relationship, what phrase is it that you instinctively know is the right response? It's not "And I value your friendship," it's not "Super, because I'm having the time of my life," and it sure as heck is not "Hey, who doesn't?"

The only fully correct response to "I love you" is "I love you, too." And it frequently slips out even when it is not fully true (though sometimes it may be true enough for the moment, if you catch my drift). Again, this is the power of being desired, and asking for the job, pointedly telling the interviewer that you want the job, is one of the strongest closes you can use.

I'm not saying that a strong close will overcome a weak resume or lack of interviewing preparation and practice. I'm not saying it will get you a job for which you're not qualified. But I *am* saying that the fact that you clearly and directly expressed your desire to be hired is guaranteed to stick in the interviewer's mind when he makes the final hiring decision. It's another factor in your favor, and using every one at your disposal is what a winning job interview is all about.

The diagram on the next page will give you a good overview of the two paths to closing an interview.

Some Essentials to Remember

As the interview winds down and you are focusing on asking good questions, using trial closes, uncovering and overturning objections, and asking for the job, it is sometimes too easy to overlook the basics. These are eye contact, a smile, and a strong handshake.

Because you will have anticipated possible objections to your candidacy before the interview, you will have had time to come up with some strategies to deal with them. Thus, when you are in the closing phase of the interview, you shouldn't look as though you are painfully struggling to dredge up the date of the Magna Carta or the ratio of whiskey to sweet vermouth in a Manhattan (1215 and 3:1, respectively). No lip-biting or squinting into space. Relax, breathe smoothly, and make good eye contact to communicate your earnestness and desire.

Your smile should come naturally because, after all, the interview is over. (Just don't sigh deeply and say "whew" under your breath.) A good, solid, dry, firm handshake will end the interview on a strong note. If your hands have perspired during the interview, subtly deal with this before that final handshake. During your interview prep sessions, try out your handshake on your practice partner a few times until you get it right. You're going for firm, not bone-crushing, and enthusiastic, not game show winner.

Closing the Interview

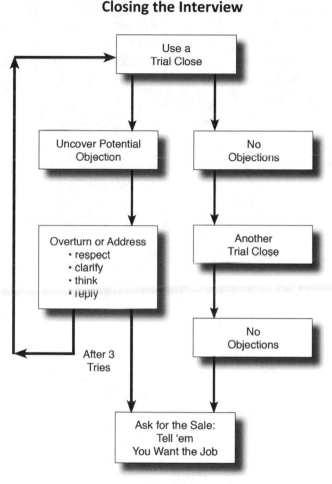

Figure 7.1

Back to Carnegie Hall

Like it or not, using effective sales techniques is essential to job hunting and job interviewing. But even the strongest salespeople I know do not automatically transfer these skills into their job interviews. However, from their experience they know enough to practice. Good questions to ask, subtle trial closes, and strategies to overcome possible objections do not just materialize out of thin air during the interview itself. They are pondered, written down, analyzed, practiced, refined, and practiced again well before the interview.

I don't expect these techniques to come to you automatically. That is why tools #10, #11, and #14 in The Good to Great Interview Toolkit all have elements touching on effective interview-closing techniques. If you practice them, you will reduce your interview anxiety, improve your interview performance, and out-prepare your competition. You may just land the job you love.

Chapter 8

Getting the Deal Done

Many job hunters make the mistake of letting down their guard and reducing their energy level and focus once they have a job offer in hand. This is quite understandable because just getting to this critical point has required quite a bit of energy and focus. This is a strategic error, however, because the hiring process is not yet complete. Naturally, your emotions are engaged at this point: relief, thankfulness, appreciation, excitement, pride, and enthusiasm. It makes sense that you'd like to just put this difficult task behind you, but this is not the time to let your emotions rule the day. You need to stay cool, collected, and focused on getting the best deal you can. And in this chapter I will teach you how to do just that.

Getting a job offer is not like winning the lottery; you're not supposed to act all surprised or speechless or gushing with emotion. The offer is a predictable result of your well-thought-out, four-front job campaign, your meticulous preparation, and a great job interview. With the work you have put into your plan and the preparation you have put into your interview, the job offer should come as no great surprise. And because it doesn't come as a bolt out of the blue, your reaction will be calm, thoughtful, and professional. But don't break out the bubbly just yet, because you still have some work to do.

The offer will most likely be made verbally at the end of the interview or in a follow-up meeting or telephone call. Your initial reaction should be appropriately pleased and appreciative, but you need to be on your guard not to say anything that could be interpreted as an immediate acceptance. It may feel as if you're supposed to immediately accept or reject the offer, but, in fact, you are not yet in a position to do because you don't know the details of the offer. You haven't sufficiently analyzed the job itself nor have you evaluated the compensation package. Your potential new employer has taken enough time to interview a series of people, think through the decision to hire you, and put this offer together. Certainly you deserve adequate time to make an informed decision.

Most employers and most recruiters understand that you need time to make a decision about the job offer, but they will subtly exert some pressure on you to make a decision "as soon as you can." From their perspective this is a reasonable approach, because they have work that needs to be done, and they think you are the person to do it, and if you aren't going to accept the offer, they need to approach their backup candidate in the shortest time period possible. Although I want you to take enough time to make an informed decision, I also want you to make it "as soon as you can" so that no one (an internal or last-minute candidate) slips in there ahead of you. You can narrow down this critical time period substantially if you lay the foundation for your decision-making *now*, before you're on the hot seat with a clock ticking loudly in your ear.

The Ticking Clock

If the job offer has been made in person or by phone, it is entirely appropriate to ask for it in writing. In fact, it's customary for the employer to have an offer package already prepared or ready to send to you. Until you have the offer letter in your hand, you have no offer. I know this seems harsh, but this is business, and not many businesses in this day and age consider a phone call or a conversation an agreement, and certainly not a contract. They know this, and now you know it, too. If you get the offer *verbally*, you can say something such as, "That's great, Barbara. I'm really looking forward to getting something in hand so I can discuss it at home and make a decision. What kind of deadline are we working with?"

If you need more time, this is the time to ask for it. You might also add something such as, "As soon as I have the offer, you can rest assured that it will be my top priority." Once the clock is ticking, your goal is to *beat the deadline*. You don't want your new employer to feel that you're holding out until the last minute just because you can.

If you are *handed* the offer letter at the end of the interview, you may say something such as, "Thank you, Barbara. I can't wait to share the good news at home. What kind of deadline are we working with?" Again, your goal is to beat the deadline, although you have less time to evaluate the offer, because you're already holding it in your hot little hands.

A number of single folks have asked me if it isn't a little weird for them to mention sitting down at home to share or discuss a job offer as a way of buying a little time to make an informed decision. Not at all; we all have some kind of family or a career coach, confidante, mentor, or advisor. For all it's anybody else's business, you could be discussing the job offer with your cat. ("Good news, Barfy; it looks like you're getting upgraded to Tender Vittles.") As of the latest issue of the *World News Weekly*, I'm assuming you were not cloned in a lab or beamed down from the mother ship, so you probably have parents or perhaps a brother or sister or crazy aunt or favorite uncle with whom you could discuss your new offer. Today there are any number of different family configurations, and whatever yours is, you get to use them to give you time to properly evaluate this job offer.

What Else Is on the Table?

A pat on the back is well-deserved at this point because all your hard work has finally paid off. But don't let up yet, because with a little extra effort on your part, you may be able to quickly generate some additional offers or negotiate with your potential new employer to improve the offer you already have in hand. Back in Chapter 3 we discussed how to get more and better interviews, and Figure 3.1 on page 66 demonstrated how the four-front job campaign is designed to help you front-end load the system so you aren't pursuing only one opportunity at a time. This is where that approach really pays off.

Generating Multiple Offers

At this point, you may have other irons in the fire. If you've played your cards right, you have already been in for a first or second interview at a couple of other places, or at least have some other good, prospective interviews coming up soon. The bona fide offer you now have gives you the opening to contact these potential employers to see if you can accelerate their hiring process. It may work or it may not, but it's worth a shot.

To put yourself in the right frame of mind to contact these folks, consider their position for a moment. They are working hard to find the right person for an open position and have identified you as a strong potential candidate. Without notifying them of your change in status, you will have reduced their pool of good job candidates, and they don't even know it. If, in fact, you are a leading candidate, their hiring process could be set back weeks, creating more recruiting and interviewing work for them and leaving the work they hoped you would be doing undone. Thus, it is actually a matter of courtesy to inform other potential employers of your situation and see if there is any way they can bring your candidacy with them to closure in a reasonable time period.

The best way to do this is with a phone call that might go something like this: "Mr. Franklin, thanks for taking my call. At the end of our last interview I know you said you were hoping to get back to me in the next couple of weeks, but there has been a new development that I wanted to bring you up to date on. Another organization that I've been in touch with has just made me a good job offer. But, as you know, I'm very interested in the position with *your* department. Now I know you have more on your plate than just filling this one job, but I was calling to see if we might be able to get together in the next couple of days."

You have courteously updated this potential new employer, you have enhanced your value in his eyes by announcing your job offer, and you have asked for another meeting to (you hope) generate another offer. Here is another instance where human psychology works in your favor. Most folks have a tendency to grasp at whatever is about to slip through their fingers. We tend to feel loss more intensely (some research says twice as much) than we do gain. At this point, you might slip through their fingers. If you are on the short list of job candidates, you will probably get the meeting and, possibly, another job offer.

Perhaps you have an interview scheduled, but it's a week or 10 days in the future. Or maybe you have no other strong job possibilities at the moment. Presumably you have been sending resumes and making inquiries to other employers that haven't yet generated interviews. Make a short list (four to six organizations) of these places and make a call similar to the previous example. Your goals are to, as a courtesy, inform them of your change in status and see if, within a reduced time frame, you can get in there for an interview.

You might try something such as, "Ms. Sizlack, I'm Amanda Huginkiz. I recently sent my resume to you about that service position you have open. [Or, "I have an upcoming interview with you about the open position in the service department."] Another organization just made me a job offer, but with everything I've learned about your company, I was really hoping to see if there might be a place for me there. I'm sure you're quite busy, but is there any way we could meet before I have to give my answer to this other company?" This is somewhat less likely to work than if you had already been in for an interview that went well. But I have seen it produce results with enough frequency to know it is something you should try, at least with some carefully targeted employers.

Don't, Don't, Don't

Never try the tactic of using one offer to leverage another if you *don't* actually have a job offer in hand. It will in all probability backfire. If you are playing fast and loose with the truth, it will probably come through in your voice. Or maybe there is nothing the interviewer can do about her hiring schedule, and now you have blown the chance for a potentially fruitful interview at a later date. Imagine how it would feel to hear something such as, "Well, Amanda, that's great about the offer. We can't really move our process along any faster and we're always sorry to lose a good potential employee. But we sure wish you the best in your new job." Gulp. What do you do now? The answer is you go away sadder but, hopefully, wiser.

Evaluating the Offer

You may or may not have had luck generating other interviews or offers. If so, this is great, because you can now balance and weigh one offer against another. But even if you have only one offer on the table, it is crucial for you to do a thorough analysis of it. You need to approach this process in a thoughtful manner and as devoid of emotion as you can. This is especially difficult if you have been unemployed for a while, because *any* paying job may seem better than being unemployed. As hard as it may be to see it at the moment, this is not true. Unless financial disaster is right around the corner, accepting the wrong job is worse than no job at all because now you have to perform well at the job you accepted while going back out into the job market to find a more suitable position. Oh, and you will need a reasonable explanation of why you are job hunting so soon after having accepted a new position. This is a hard sell and you should avoid it if humanly possible.

Two central elements of any job offer are intimately interwoven: the job itself and what they are offering to pay you to do it. It is important that you draw a clear distinction between the two so that you can assess them independently. What you are seeking is a balance between a good job that fits with your short- and long-term career goals and a compensation package that is fair for someone with your background, skills, and expertise. By making a calculated, professional, two-pronged assessment of the job offer, you can avoid jumping at a great job for which you will be underpaid (and resentful), or being swept away by a great pay package for a job that you really don't fit (and, ultimately, being miserable). Taking the time to conduct this assessment will put you in a strong position if you need to try to upgrade the position that has been offered, and it will certainly be an asset when you negotiate to enhance your compensation package. Let's take the two parts of this assessment in turn.

Analysis of the Job

I know, I know—I told you to tell them that you wanted the job when you were closing the interview, and now I'm telling you to analyze the job with the critical eye of a pawnbroker. Hey, that's the difference between selling and buying. When you were selling yourself, you were putting the best possible spin on who you are and what you can do. It was *their job* to really dig in and find out what you are all about. Now that they have made you the offer, they are selling you on the job and the organization. Now it's *your job* to really dig in and make doubly sure that this is the job and the organization in which you can succeed.

The Work Itself

In one of the great organizational studies of all time concerning employee motivation, Frederick Herzberg identified *the work itself* as being among the most powerful of workplace motivators. If the work itself is wrong for you, then no amount of money, status, car allowance, signing bonus, or anything else can make it right. You have been thinking about this job (or one like it) since you began your job hunt. You had certain criteria in your head as you began your search. Your initial research fortified this picture with hard data about where this job might be found and how much you might get paid to do it. You further explored this set of goals through your interviewing process. Now is the time to compare and contrast your goals and targets with the offer or offers you have been able to generate.

The Job Offer Analysis Tool (#15 in the Toolkit) can help you systematically think through the distinct elements of the job or jobs you have been offered. It has a number of items that will help you assess the likelihood of your success in any new position. Broadly speaking, they break out into four categories: (1) degree of fit with your current job target(s), (2) your assessment of the organization, (3) degree of fit with your career goals, and (4) how this position will affect your lifestyle. Let's take them in turn.

Fit With Your Job Target(s)

Is the job you are being offered the one you actually discussed in the interview? Will you be doing the things you most want to do? Is this job a step up or a lateral move? Are you ready for this level of responsibility? Is the scope of responsibility more or less than what you hoped it might be? Can you tell? How does it fit with your functional, industry, and geographic targets? Have you assessed your relationship with your potential supervisor, peers, and subordinates? How secure do you think this position is? Does it have the status you want? In this job, will you have adequate opportunity to develop your technical and/or management skills? How confident are you that you will succeed in this job? What don't you know about this job, and how can you find it out?

The Organization

It is possible to be offered a job that is just what you've been looking for, but the organization is so dysfunctional that despite your best efforts, you still can't succeed. To avoid this, you need to get a good overview of the entire organization. What is the history of this organization? What are the organization's prospects for the future? Has it been or could it be bought out, merged, or acquired? What would this mean for your position? What kind of reputation does the company have in the industry, with vendors, suppliers, and contractors, and in the community? What is the organizational culture? How does it treat its people? Does it typically promote from within or is it almost certain that you will have to look outside the organization to get ahead?

Fit With Your Career Goal

The job you are being offered may or may not be your dream job. So be it. The big questions are: Will this job help you on your path to ultimate career success? Is this job a step forward in your career or is it merely a stopgap assignment? Will this job allow you to develop the skills you need to succeed but don't yet have? Does this organization have a supervisory or management development program? How will this job and this employer look on your resume?

Lifestyle Issues

Your new job is going to have an impact on you and your family well beyond the parameters described in the offer letter. One lifestyle issue I hear more and more about is business travel. How much is required, and how much of it is overnight, on weekends, or international? Is this the kind of workplace where you can fly in at 10 or 11 p.m. and be expected at the office at 8:30 a.m. the next day? Do they have a "comp time" (or overtime) policy? What is the vacation policy, and are employees actually encouraged to use it? How often is relocation necessary, and what is the "relo" policy? If you have to relocate, will they help your partner or spouse find a new job? Does the company have a paternity/maternity or family leave policy? Is this organization known as family-friendly or family-unfriendly?

Are We Okay for Launch?

You have looked at this job from every angle you can think of. Perhaps you haven't been able to answer every one of the questions put forth here. Which of those questions are essential for you to have answered before giving this job a thumbs-up or thumbs-down? Where can you find this information? The library, the Web, your network contacts. Or will you need another meeting with your prospective employer?

Although this job may not be perfect, it may still be a good career move for you right now. My purpose in having you thoroughly dissect this job is for you to know its benefits and liabilities so you can make the best decision possible. I have stressed gathering and assessing hard data, but I also want you to check in with your gut—your feelings, your emotions. What are they telling you? Is this job a good one for you now or should you keep looking?

Once you have completed this assessment, you have to make one of three decisions. You may decide that this job is totally wrong for you. If so, you must reject the offer and make a courteous call thanking the interviewer for his time and interest. But don't take this path without thinking it through. You may decide that even though the job isn't perfect, perhaps you can negotiate on enough key issues so that it becomes acceptable. I think this is always worth a try; you have nothing to lose because you have almost decided to reject the offer anyway. Make a list of your bottom-line issues for your negotiation session and move on to evaluating the compensation package. My fervent hope is that you are able to decide that the job that has been offered to you is just what you are looking for. If you are, in fact, sure about the job itself, it is time to look analytically at what they are offering to pay you to do it.

Evaluating the Compensation Package

The most energetic and fortunate job hunters will have generated more than one job offer, which makes the compensation package evaluation process fairly straightforward. With more than one offer on the table, you have concrete data from one that you can directly compare with the other(s). This makes the decision process a bit easier. At the other end of the spectrum is the job hunter who is unemployed and may be having serious financial problems. Her analysis is going to be pretty easy, too. (Let's see now, eating versus starving...what to do, what to do?) Fortunately, most folks aren't in this position or are, at least, a few steps away from it. In fact, even if you are feeling financially strapped, I want you to take some time to fully understand your new compensation package.

What most job hunters face is a situation in which they are generating job offers one at a time, regardless of whether they are employed or not. This tends to lead most folks to narrow down the decision criteria to two: current/most recent pay vs. new offer. To make your compensation evaluation process as unemotional and business-like as possible, I always advise that you invest some time and energy *before* you generate your first offer to expand your decision criteria. The Compensation Package Evaluation Tool (#16 in the Toolkit) shows you how to do this.

I want you to compile some specific compensation data well before you generate your first job offer. Start by documenting the elements of your current pay plan. Then, based on the target(s) of your job hunt, determine what you want your new compensation package to look like. Next, I want you to engage in a very enlightening exercise: evaluate your current cost of living and financial needs (not *wants*) and determine what is the minimum compensation package that you can afford to accept.

This latter set of data is important to have for a couple of reasons. Sometimes you're offered a dream job, but at a much lower salary than had been targeted. As long as it doesn't lead to financial ruin (that is, cash flow below your cost of living), accepting this offer might be a good decision if it launches you into a great new career or relocates you to where you've always wanted to live. Financial planners have told me that this is also a useful exercise to help a family determine how much they can really set aside for a secure financial future rather than just burning up pay raises with the purchase of unneeded consumer goods.

Even if you are generating only one job offer at a time, you now have three other compensation packages against which you can compare the one you just received. Some of the compensation elements you see in Tool #16 may not apply to you. There may be some that are unique to your situation that you need to include. But now you have a customized, data-rich tool that can help you make a thoughtful decision about the compensation package you have been offered that minimizes some of the emotional aspects of financial discussions.

If the compensation package being offered is not up to what you have set as a target, do not despair. Using your evaluation tool, determine what salary and benefits comprise your bottom line. Add 5 to 10 percent to this and you now have your starting negotiating position. It's good to remember that although most job hunters are hoping for a 20-percent boost in salary, this won't automatically happen just because you are changing jobs. Even if the pay you are being offered is on target with what you had hoped to get, I recommend that you also add 5 to 10 percent to that number and try to negotiate the offer upward. You may have underestimated the market or the demand for people in your specialty, and it is likely that you were offered a salary somewhere near the middle of the pay range for your position. Either way, you may be able to generate some wiggle room that will put more money in your pocket.

So You Want...?

Before you contact the person who made you the offer start negotiating, I want you to have a crystal-clear picture of your negotiating position. Do not go into this thinking you can wing it. They have a lot more practice at this than you do. You have done a comprehensive analysis of the job that has been offered. What do you need to accept the job? What are going to ask for? What are you willing to live without?

You have evaluated all the elements of the compensation package. You know there is probably more money on the table if you are willing to ask for it. What is the number you are looking for? What else are you going to ask for? What is the minimum you are willing to accept to do this job?

Take the time to write down the short list of items you want to negotiate. Tell yourself that you are worth what you are asking for. Having a positive, upbeat attitude will help you as you negotiate. You are not going in to beat anyone out of anything. You are looking only for what the market will bear and to do what is best for your career and your family. Regardless of how successful you are in your negotiations, employers understand and accept this.

Negotiating—The Short Course

Negotiations of any kind are always most effective when done face-to-face. This enables you to see and read facial expressions, monitor changes in body language, and better interpret changes in vocal tone and inflection. You do all of these things almost unconsciously in your everyday conversations, but these data are critical in negotiating so you can better assess what to push for, when to push for it, and how far to push. As I said before, do not go into a negotiating session looking to beat the other person. A "win-lose" attitude will not help you achieve your end goal and can potentially poison your future working relationship. Think "win-win," and it will positively influence your attitude, demeanor, and approach.

The Do's and Don'ts of Negotiating a Job Offer

DON'T:	Be lazy or look unprofessional. Negotiating is expected.
DO:	Practice your negotiating skills beforehand.
DON'T:	Walk in blind/unprepared.
DO:	Use your contacts, social media, and salary Websites to learn ahead of time salary ranges and typical compensation packages.
DON'T:	Fear or hesitate to ask for what you're worth.
DO:	Realize that settling for something less will cause you increasing job dissatisfaction with time.
DON'T:	Talk about what you "need." That's your issue, not theirs.
DO:	Talk about what you will bring to the assignment, your assessment of a strong fit, and your eagerness to join the team and get to work.
DON'T:	Immediately accept the first offer.
DO:	Learn what the salary range is and know there is probably some flexibility.
DON'T:	Throw out hard salary numbers first or too early.
DO:	Keep it as general/vague as you can for as long as you can. Speak in ranges (for example, high 50s, mid-80s, low 70s).
DON'T:	Immediately reject an offer that looks unacceptable.
DO:	Take the time to use the Good to Great Interview Tools #15 and #16 to thoroughly evaluate the job itself and the compensation package.
DON'T:	Ask for the moon or try to negotiate every item.
DO:	Identify the top two or three items that, if enhanced, would make the offer acceptable. Pick your battles. Negotiate them in order of importance.
DON'T:	Get miffed, personally offended, or visibly frustrated, and don't burn any bridges.
DO:	Realize this is just how business is done. You may or may not be able to successfully negotiate the offer to your satisfaction. You may or may not ultimately decide to accept the best offer they can make. But keep your reputation as a professional intact because it is a small world and you will run into these people again.

Figure 8.1

First Things First

When you meet to discuss your job offer, start by thanking the interviewer for the opportunity to discuss the offer with him. Although most folks want to jump right to the money issue, address the most important job issues first, because you want to be seen as being more interested in succeeding at the job than you are in the money. Once you have the essentials of duties and responsibilities, reporting relationships, staff, resources, and such taken care of, you can then address the compensation package.

You have already identified what it is you are looking for, but it requires a little finesse to get to the point. I suggest you recap all the job issues you have already agreed upon and then segue into the money issue. You might say something such as, "That's great, Jeff. Working directly for you to open up three new call centers in the next 18 months, two of which I'll end up running myself, is just the kind of assignment I've been looking for." At this point, ol' Jeff is nodding his head positively, agreeing with your description of the job and expressing satisfaction at having found someone who is such a great fit for it. Then you add something such as, "I'm really looking forward to the opportunity and I'm confident that I'm the right person for this job, but as I looked over the offer, I was hoping that there might be some flexibility in the compensation."

Now Jeff doesn't think you mean flexibility for them to pay you *less*; he knows you mean flexibility for them to pay you *more*. What's great about an approach like this is that you can use it whether or not you genuinely need more money before you can accept the job. Even if the pay is fine with you, most employers always leave a little financial wiggle room, expect you to be savvy enough to try to find it, and will respect you for your effort. For you to disappoint them would almost be, well, uncivilized. So go for it. This employer now has a vested interest in closing this deal with you, and usually, a little more money can be forthcoming.

Jeff might say something such as, "Well, Alyona, what salary did you have in mind?" or, "Okay, Alyona, what's your bottom line?" At this point, it's time to fish or cut bait. Say the number you have in mind. This number should be realistic and based on your earlier research about the field, the function, and this company. Jeff will say one of three things. He will say something such as, "Okay, we can do that," or, "I'm not sure we can do that. I'll need to find out," or, "Wow, we have a problem because we can't get anywhere near that."

It's great news if he gives the first response, although your immediate, natural reaction will be, "D'oh. I should have asked for more." Sorry, Homer, that bus just left and the deal is done. The second response is sort of like a maybe. Treat it as a temporary detour. Say something such as, "Great. I appreciate your looking into that for me because we're not really that far apart." Then drop the topic for this discussion, but, before you leave, end with, "Can I expect a call on the salary issue?" to show you haven't forgotten about it. If you get the message that you are miles apart, it still may not be a deal-breaker, but you have some fancy footwork ahead of you.

Putting the Deal Together

You may need to ask the question bluntly, "So how far apart are we?" Whatever the number is, don't give up the ship. Try to discover if there is an incentive program or a bonus plan based on performance that could bridge the gap. Explore the extent and value of each item in the benefit plan. You may be pleasantly surprised to learn that an employer matching 401(k) plan, company car or car allowance, or other benefits (that is, family dental coverage, or tennis, golf, or health club membership) more than makes up the difference, given how benefits are treated by the tax laws. The key is to always stay positive that the deal can be worked out, and always keep throwing ideas on the table. If you are at the high end of the salary range for the job in question, ask if the job can be upgraded so you can be at the lower end of the next range. Ask if a signing bonus is possible. Ask if a three- or six-month performance and salary review might be possible. If you don't get defensive and are able to treat this as just another business problem for two motivated people to solve, your attractiveness will only increase.

You may get asked something such as, "What is the minimum you would accept?" Do your best to stay away from absolute numbers. I'd try something such as, "My compensation [remember, that's salary plus the value of your benefits package] is now in the high 40s, and I'd need something in the low 50s to make this move." Using vague terms such as "low 50s," "mid-60s," or "high 70s" can help you move a financial step ahead without having your interviewer feel that you are delivering an ultimatum. Ultimatums are always a bad negotiating strategy because very few people like to be leveraged by overt pressure. You want the interviewer to feel that she is directing this process with the ultimate goal of securing your services for the organization. Your role in this process is to help open up every possible avenue to achieve this end.

Unless you are a professional diplomat or labor arbitrator, this negotiating process will feel foreign to you. Before you go in to negotiate your offer, prepare some phrases you think will help you. I've used many of them in this chapter; go back and underline the ones you want to try out. Try them out on your interview practice partner until you find a few that feel comfortable. Role-play asking for what you deserve. It's a good skill to develop in all areas of your life

Accepting or Rejecting

Figure 8.2 on the next page gives a systematic overview of how you can best handle the job offers you have so diligently generated. Think about how much time, energy, hard work, and emotional investment it takes to generate one good offer. This is why each and every job offer must be handled with care and professionalism, and be given the respect due a rare and valuable resource. Given the significance of this element of your job hunt, let's quickly review the steps in managing the job offer process:

1. Ask for the decision time frame and bargain for more.
2. Prospect for other offers or interviews.
3. Analyze the job.
4. Evaluate the compensation.
5. Set negotiating targets for the job and for the compensation.
6. Negotiate (in person is best).
7. Decide (accept or reject the offer).

You should communicate your acceptance or rejection of the job offer as soon as you have a firm decision. Your potential employer needs to know if this recruiting and employment task is completed so he can plan for your integration into the rest of the work team or if he needs to start pursuing other candidates. Do your best to beat the decision deadline rather than waiting until the last minute.

Accepting the offer is easy. You do it after deciding that the initial offer is acceptable or after successfully negotiating an improved offer. In person is best, of course, but a phone call will suffice. Try for the personal touch so you can show your enthusiasm. Don't treat your acceptance

Handling Offers

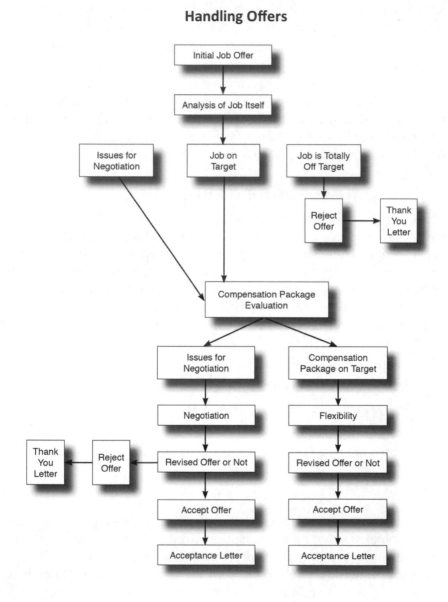

Figure 8.2

lightly by leaving a text, voice mail, or e-mail. Follow up your verbal acceptance with a formal letter that outlines the terms and conditions of your employment and clarifies your start date.

Rejecting a job offer is a little trickier. There are two points at which you can make your rejection decision: either at the point of deciding that the job itself is totally wrong for you, or after unsuccessfully negotiating either the job itself or the compensation package. Although no one likes to deliver bad news on a one-on-one basis, I encourage you to suck it up and talk to the interviewer directly. Convey that this is a business, not a personal, decision; say you're sorry things didn't work out; and thank the interviewer for her time and interest. Do not get drawn into an extended conversation about your decision unless the interviewer is offering to improve the job offer to meet your needs. In the unlikely event that this happens, as with all job offers, ask when you can get it in writing. Do not express anything negative about the job or the company. The company made you the best offer it could, and it was you who decided not to take it. Do not give the interviewer any negative feedback at all; your rejection is all the bad news she needs for today. Try to leave the conversation on a warm, personal, and appreciative note, because, trust me, you will bump into her or someone she knows later on in your career, and you want her final perception of you to be courteous and professional, not snide or snippy. Follow up with a nonspecific but appreciative letter thanking her for her time, and express the hope that you may get to work together at a later date.

Start Spreadin' the News

Another of my counterintuitive rules for going from a good job hunter to a great job hunter is that now, the time between when you accept your new job and the time you actually start it, is a great time to lay the foundation for your next job search. No, I don't mean you should go out and start looking for a new job tomorrow; I mean that how you close out your current job hunt will strongly influence how long it will take and how much energy it will take to get you up and running on your next job search, regardless of when it comes to pass.

Compile or clean up your list of all the contacts you made during your job hunt. This includes everyone in your physical contact network, your social media contacts and the people they introduced you to, your reference librarian helpers, every recruiter you contacted (regardless of whether they helped you or not; maybe next time they will), the facilitators of every job-search support group you attended, your job references, the Webmaster for every career Website you used, every professional or technical association whose job listings you used, the company recruiting managers you contacted, and everyone with whom you interviewed. In short, this is your new, improved, and expanded career network. Capture every bit of useful data you've come across. Never again will your career file and contact network be as short, as small, or as thin as it was when you started this job hunt.

Prepare a letter that will go to this list of people that thanks them for all their help during your recent job search. Also, inform any recruiters you reached out to (even those who didn't respond or help); you want them to update your profile in their database. Obviously, you'll need to personalize this letter for your most helpful and supportive contacts. Let everyone know what job you landed and how they can contact you. Send this mailing about a week after you have started your new job—no sense jinxing things at this point, eh?

Shortly after you start your new job, make a contact in the marketing or public relations department and see if it is appropriate to compile a press release to send to the business press, professional associations, or even just your hometown newspaper. Remember to update your social media profile. You have just achieved success in a demanding and competitive process, and you deserve all the recognition you can get. This, of course, raises your professional profile and will contribute to the continued success of your career. The Job Search Wrap-Up Tool (#18 in the Toolkit) will help you conclude this job search professionally as you lay a solid foundation for your next one.

Chapter 9

Damage Control

Some Obvious (and Not-So-Obvious) Tips to Overcome Job-Hunting Mistakes, Glitches, Potholes, and Idiots

THROUGHOUT THIS BOOK I HAVE SHARED MY OPTIMISM IN YOUR ULTIMATE CAREER SUCCESS, MY ENTHUSIASM FOR YOUR JOB HUNT, AND MY CONFIDENCE IN YOUR ABILITY TO DEVELOP INTO A GREAT JOB INTERVIEWER. I have counseled you to invest considerable energy in your job hunt. I have showed you how to control your interview anxiety at every step of the process. I have prodded you to take ultimate responsibility for your job-hunting and job-interviewing success. At every turn I have urged you to take the high road. I have tried my best to motivate you, as the old song goes, to "accentuate the positive." This is because a can-do attitude can make all the difference between an engaging job and a career that you love and the majority of employees who endure sad work lives of dissatisfaction that spills over onto every other aspect of their lives.

At this point, however, I should point out that the path to success in every challenging human endeavor is littered with mistakes, glitches, errors, oversights, and the occasional idiot pointing in the wrong direction. This is why pencils have erasers, cars have a reverse gear, and boats have life jackets. The question isn't *if* mistakes will happen or *if* obstacles will appear; the question is *when* they will happen and *how* you will deal with them.

When I meet with job hunters to debrief them over a couple of celebratory drinks after a successful job search, the greatest laughter usually emerges from the things that didn't go so well—the errors, the mistakes, the glitches. They occur in every job hunt, and yours will be no different. The key here is to take everything in stride, prepare for as many eventualities as you can, and, when faced with an interview predicament, stay positive and give it your best shot. You don't have to be perfect; you only have to be better than the other candidates for this one particular job. By sorting out how you will deal with potential problems ahead of time, again, you, will be out-preparing your competition.

With luck, you may never run into an interview format you're not familiar with, be asked trick questions, stumble badly in an interview, or meet up with the dreaded idiot interviewer. But my approach isn't about luck; it's about you being able to fix any job-hunting mistake you make along the way and turn any interview into a great job interview, regardless of any pothole or calamity you may encounter.

Blowing Your Cover

You must be cautious if you are job hunting while employed. As I mentioned earlier, perhaps you are one of a lucky minority who has a boss who realizes Lincoln freed the slaves and that any career-savvy employee should always be assessing his or her value in today's job marketplace. But many bosses resent it and may act punitively when they discover a subordinate is job hunting. Here are a few ways to avoid alerting your boss to your job search.

➻ **Do not show lack of interest in your current assignment.** Looking for new ways to contribute is one thing, but avoiding the basic elements of your job is a dead giveaway that you've already "psychologically resigned."

➻ **Do not withdraw socially.** Keep up your water cooler, coffee room, cafeteria, and break room relationships. You need to stay in the informal communication loop while you're still there, and withdrawing from colleagues just because you're looking to bail out is a bad networking strategy for the long run.

➥ **Do not let down your guard**. Some who you think are your friends are really only work acquaintances; some may even be covert competitors. Keep your own counsel.

➥ **Don't leave a digital trail**. Use your own electronics for voice mail, e-mail, and text messages.

➥ **Don't click your way out of your current job**. Use privacy settings if you are updating your job status on social media or adding multiple recruiter and HR types as contacts.

➥ **Don't complain your way out of your current job**. No negative comments about your job, boss, the company, or your colleagues. Not only will you burn bridges, but prospective employers will get wind of it, and nobody likes a Debby Downer.

➥ **Don't slack your way out of your current job**. We get it that you don't love this job anymore. But leaving with high marks and a flourish not only shows class, but it also helps you to protect your job reference—a valuable asset for all future job hunts.

Typical Mistakes of Older Job Hunters

If you are mid-career or older and you'd like a nice motivational plug about your many strengths, go to *www.drpaulpowers.com*, click on *LifeMap* (which is an archive of my e-newsletter to which you may subscribe for free), and scroll down to the 10/13 edition, *The Strengths of Older Workers/Older Job Hunters*. But I have also seen some older job hunters trip over their own feet in a current job hunt. Here are some common mistakes that I've observed and how to avoid them.

➥ **Your resume makes you look older than you are**. You need only go back 10–15 years. Today's resume is technology driven. Before a human being reads your resume, it has to get through applicant tracking systems (ATS), which search for specific keywords for hard skills, soft skills, geography, tech skills, education, and so on. The best place to find appropriate keywords are in the job postings to which you are responding. Use standard fonts and standard headings; nothing fancy. Go online and you'll find more suggestions in this vein.

➻ **You're socially invisible.** In Chapter 3 there is an entire section devoted to the Obvious and Not-So-Obvious Social Media Job-Hunting Mistakes. Being invisible is #1 and it applies to many more older folks than young folks; it's dangerous because it suggests that you are behind the times. If you skimmed that section on social media and social networking in Chapter 3, go back over it now.

➻ **You act old.** You don't show energy—in your face, in your eyes, in your step. Don't collapse into your seat with a sigh or a groan. I'm not suggesting you bound into the office like a golden retriever, but act alive and show that you're glad to be there.

➻ **You're not considering other options.** Sure, you probably want a full-time job, but what about a consulting gig or a contracting job or a challenging temp assignment? If it leads to developing new skills, new experiences, and new contacts, why not consider it instead of dismissing it out of hand?

➻ **You're not practicing your interviewing skills.** Sure, you've done this dozens of times before, but how recently? Your experience can give you a leg up, but not if you don't polish your approach. Your competition is practicing right now.

➻ **You're not learning anything new.** Read widely, be aware of popular culture, take a course, and try out a new physical activity, charitable group, or hobby. These kinds of things show that you are adaptable, flexible, and enjoy trying and learning new things. You don't need a nose ring, but a good part of not looking too old is keeping an open, curious outlook.

➻ **You're waiting for something to happen.** Patience is a virtue everywhere—except in job hunting. You are wasting valuable time you could be investing in productive job-hunting activities. Use either Tool #1 or Tool #17 in The Good to Great Interview Toolkit to get your job search moving forward.

Typical Mistakes of Younger Job Hunters

After beating up on job hunters my own age, you didn't think I'd let younger folks off easy, did you? One of the best things about young folks in general is that they are typically optimistic (seeing the glass as half full) and energetic (willing to do whatever it takes to get the job done). These qualities alone make them very attractive job candidates. But these very traits (and a few others I mention in the following list) can sometimes work to a younger job hunter's detriment. Here are some common mistakes that I've observed and how to avoid them.

- **Not using your career office.** You or your parents have paid a ton of dough for college, so use every resource at your disposal. The career savviest students have been using it to uncover great internships since freshman year. The career office can help you polish that resume to a clean, well-written marketing document, teach interview skills, and sometimes introduce you to helpful alumni.
- **Not cleaning up your social media profile.** Do not rely on privacy settings. Unless you're trying to land a job as beer taster, bong manufacturer, or Hawaiian Tropic model, dump *all* those pictures. Review the Chapter 3 section on the Obvious and Not-So-Obvious Social Media Job-Hunting Mistakes. Oh, and no more stupid "hi mom, I'm a rapper" voice-mail greetings. You're an adult now—get used to it.
- **Not keeping Mom and Dad at arm's length.** Ask for their advice and maybe some initial contacts. Give them periodic updates and let it go at that. If you're not motivated enough to go out and get a job on your own, no amount of harping or meddling is going to help. Be aware that career experts like me are telling your folks not to let you live with them rent-free indefinitely. You (and your folks) will be amazed at the motivational impact of room-and-board payments and moving-out timetables.
- **Not doing rigorous research.** This isn't a book report that you're trying to sleaze by on. Taking a quick scan of Wikipedia or a company's annual report is not adequate pre-interview research. Get busy and read *everything* you can find on any potential employer that is willing to take the time to interview you. This includes news reports in the mass media as well

as industry publications, Twitter feeds, and asking for other information sources from anybody within your social media network.

→ **Holding out for your dream job**. Get real. Nobody starts at the top. Mommy and Daddy, your soccer coach, your violin teacher, or your main squeeze may think you're the best thing since sliced bread, but there's competition out there that is smarter, better prepared, and harder working. Hold onto that dream, but to achieve it in the world of work, you've first got to get in the game. Focus on landing that entry-level job or your first job in a new field. Realism is your friend; an over-inflated ego is not.

→ **Relying too much on technology and not enough on human beings**. In Chapter 3, I showed all the wonderful ways today's technology explosion can help you get a job. But employers don't hire electronic profiles or resumes; they hire people. Do not shrink from face-to-face networking even if it makes you uncomfortable. This is probably the avenue that will lead to your new job.

→ **Forgetting your manners.** *Please* and *thank you* alone won't get you the job, but forgetting them can prevent you from ever getting it. Sometimes your anxiety or focus can keep you from looking like a pleasant person who others would want to see every day and work with. Civility and courtesy is due to *everybody* you encounter, from the parking attendant to the folks in the lobby or elevator and *all* administrative support people. One word from any of them that you're a rude jerk will deep six your chances for sure. Your interviewer is the gatekeeper between you and a job you want. Express genuine appreciation for his or her time and assert a clear interest in the job as well as your hope that you'll be hired.

Unusual Interview Formats

Thus far, the only interview format we've addressed is the face-to-face, one-on-one interview. There are a few others you need to be prepared for.

One Ringy Dingy

Another common interview format is the telephone interview. It is often used as a tool to screen applicants before a face-to-face meeting is scheduled. This is standard practice for both contingency recruiters and retained search consultants. Because you use your phone every day for mundane purposes, it is easy to take this interview casually. Huge mistake! You're not ordering Chinese food here, bucko; you're trying to get your foot in the door with an important job target. This phone meeting is as important as a face-to-face meeting because if you don't do well in the first one, you won't even get to try the other.

The two keys to mastering the phone interview are preparation and physical setting. Before your phone interview, review your research notes, your resume, and the short list of questions you want to ask. Have a clean pad of paper ready and put the interviewer's name and title on it. That way you won't use the wrong name (easy to do when you're not actually looking at someone), and you'll have a convenient place to take notes. If an unexpected call for a phone interview comes in, try to reschedule it. Say you were just on your way out for a meeting. You wouldn't go into a face-to-face interview on the spur of the moment, so why would you wing it now? Even if you bump the call back another 10 or 20 minutes, you will be that much better prepared.

Speakerphones are great as long as they don't make you sound as if you were underwater or on a police bullhorn. If you have a speakerphone, try it out on someone who will give you brutally honest feedback before you ever use it in an interview. If yours sounds clear and crisp, use it, because it will allow you to take notes and use your hands to gesture with as you speak. You may not have noticed it before, but hand gestures and facial expressions add variety to your voice and make you sound more engaged and easier to listen to. I know this may sound corny, but you may want to take a lesson from successful telemarketers and keep a mirror on your desk to remind you to smile. A person on one end of the phone can tell when the person on the other end is smiling, because smiling uses muscles that change the tone of one's voice for the better. As with video interviews (which we'll cover a bit later), I suggest you write the words "smile" and "breathe" on a sticky note and post it where it will jog your memory.

Using a speakerphone presupposes that you have a private, quiet place from which to make and take phone calls. I have never had an interviewer tell me that listening to a screaming baby, yapping dog, or whining vacuum cleaner made a job candidate sound more professional. It may induce pity, but not a job offer.

I don't care what promises your cell phone carrier alleges; their service is not 100-percent reliable. Coverage may sometimes be good, it may sometimes be great, but it is not 100-percent dependable. Thus, *never* conduct a phone interview (or, God forbid, a negotiating session) on a cell phone. Imagine your panic after answering a question brilliantly only to hear your interviewer saying, "Are you still there? Can you hear me? Are you there? Hello?" Again, most of these are little points to help you sound more attractive to a potential employer, but all these little points can add up in your favor or nibble away at your success.

Just Like *Star Trek*

As the cost of video conferencing technology has come down and the quality has improved, more organizations are using it in the hiring process. It is time-efficient, saves on travel expenses, and allows for the screening of more candidates and candidates from remote locations. If used effectively, it can improve the quality of the interviewing and hiring process. Because it requires preparation on the hiring side of the equation, often a uniform set of questions is prepared that will be asked of all candidates, thus increasing the fairness of the process. Interviews can be recorded and reviewed later for a more accurate comparison of how candidates answered identical questions without relying on vague impressions, illegible notes, or faulty memories.

Some organizations use video interview companies, but an increasing number of employers and recruiters use Skype. One recent study showed that the number of job candidates having video interviews is doubling every two years. I expect that this trend will continue, so you'll need to develop your know-how and skills in this area.

If your computer does not have video and voice capability, it is time for an upgrade. If this is impossible, try to find a local employment center, college, library, family member, or friend that has a video-friendly computer you can use in privacy. Here are some ideas to help you master this technology.

Before the video interview:

→ Practice. Use your own Webcam or find someone else's to use to assess and adjust your overall appearance, demeanor, mannerisms, eye contact, and voice. Make sure the camera is not pointing right up your nose! Adjust the lighting: a little bit bright is good, but avoid too much from behind or the sides, which can give that *Twilight Zone* look.

➤➤ My podcasting friends suggest not using the camera and microphone built in your computer. You can find a set-up with an HD camera, microphone, mic holder, and tripod for less than $100 at online retailers.

➤➤ When practicing, use the picture-in-picture feature (small image in the corner of the chat window) so that you can see what the other end is seeing. But just before the interview, disable this feature so it won't distract you or cover it up with the previously mentioned sticky note reading breathe/relax.

➤➤ Plan your attire as you would for any interview. Dressing appropriately helps you feel the part. Avoid busy patterns and stick to neutral colors. Don't assume that only your top half will be seen. What if you need to get up for a document or adjust the equipment?

➤➤ If interviewing from home, remove from the camera's view anything that anyone might consider inappropriate for a business interview.

➤➤ Send any requested materials well in advance of the interview (for example, resume, application form, portfolio pieces, and so on).

➤➤ Review any video instructions you've been given and feel free to ask for help with anything you don't understand.

➤➤ Clear your desk or workstation of clutter, distractions, and anything that might make noise or distract the interviewer. Having a few (not-so-obvious) notes is one of the benefits of this type of interview. Just don't pick them up and read aloud from them.

➤➤ Arrange to be in place early to ensure that everything is working and to relax a bit.

During the video interview:

➤➤ Feel free to ask for a quick review of the equipment.

➤➤ Ask if you can be clearly seen and heard.

➤ Confirm that they have any materials you have sent. Have back-ups ready to go, just in case.

➤ Stay cool if the system freezes up. Reboot your system and wait for them to call back. After five or 10 minutes, you can try reaching them. Technical difficulties can happen; it's how you deal with them that counts. Watch the salty language.

➤ Look at the camera; this is the video equivalent of eye contact. If you look down at your screen, keyboard, or desk, all they will see is the top of your head.

➤ Don't fidget, check e-mail, play with paperclips, click your pen, or make any distracting noises the microphone will pick up.

➤ Use active listening (your shrink does). Responses such as "Uh-huh," "I see," "That's interesting," and "hmm" let the interviewer know that you're paying attention and that the equipment is working.

➤ Use hand gestures sparingly because on video they can be distracting. For emphasis, use vocal/tonal variety.

➤ Before signing off, ask about next steps and then express thanks and appreciation as you would for any interview.

After the video interview:

➤ Double and triple check to make sure the equipment is turned off.

➤ Do a post-interview review as you would with any interview. An invaluable tool for this, if your system has one, is a Record feature.

➤ Plan for how you will improve your video interviewing performance.

➤ Send a thank-you note as you would for any interview.

The final points here should reinforce that a video interview is not much different from an in-person interview, but is just as important. I've heard it said that a video interview can be *more* important than a traditional, face-to-face screening interview because your performance can be reviewed, compared, and assessed more rigorously. Mastering this technology and this process is one more way you can out-prepare your competition and improve your interviewing skills from good to great.

The Group Grope

They're really called panel interviews, and I truly dislike them. (I have to learn not to repress my true feelings.) You meet with a group of three or more interviewers, and each of them takes a turn asking you questions. Not completely unlike the Spanish Inquisition. Sometimes all of them are interested in every answer, sometimes some of them are interested in all of the answers, sometimes some of them are interested in some of the answers, and sometimes they are only interested in the answer to the question they asked. And sometimes there's a poor sap in there who doesn't know why he's there or what he's interested in because he only showed up because his boss told him to sit in. So you don't know who wants to hear what. You'll end up directing your answer to the person who asked the question while looking around and trying to make some eye contact with the others who seem interested without having your head swivel around like that girl in *The Exorcist*.

Although you know who arranged the interview and who is likely to be your boss, it is impossible to know the relationships (personal or reporting) among all of them. Sometimes there will be people in a panel interview who have competing agendas or different ideas of what they are looking for, or even disagreements on the dimensions of the job itself. Because they should have worked all this out ahead of time, it is a huge waste of their time. And, of course, it is insane to think some Gandhi-like outsider will miraculously appear and bridge all the spoken and unspoken conflicts in one meeting. But, to paraphrase the popular bumper sticker, stuff happens, and it may happen to you.

If you learn beforehand that you are in for a panel interview, do your best to find out who is participating, why they are participating, and what, if any, specific interest they have in how this job is filled. If something like this is sprung on you when you arrive for the interview (which already gives you some not-so-great feedback about the organization), make it your first agenda to go around the room asking for (and writing down) people's names and titles. Be pleasant about it (because you can't do anything about it anyway), expressing pleasure in meeting them, and, if you can manage it, ask each of them how they or their department will be involved with the person to be hired. If you're able to do this, you can probably tailor your responses appropriately. If you end up answering questions pretty much in the dark about whose agenda is what, just play it straight down the middle and hope for the best.

The Cattle Call

As grim as this interview sounds, it's a heck of a lot better than the group grope. The formal name is the serial interview—you complete one interview and then move right on to someone else. Typically, this doesn't happen until a second or later interview, but if you find yourself being walked down the hall to meet someone else after your first interview, you can bet it's good news for you. Either somebody else saw your resume, was impressed, and asked to see you when you came in, or that person told your interviewer to bring you around if she was impressed enough to think about hiring you.

Serial interviews are draining, but they are a great opportunity for using your job interview skills. It is important to keep your energy level high because you are actually making a series of first impressions. As in the panel interview, the key is to get a quick read on who these people are, what their agenda is, and why they are interested in this new hire. You can ask similar questions of multiple folks, and as you think about the answers afterward, you will learn a lot about the organization. Remember to ask each person for his or her card so you have the correct information to send personalized follow-up letters.

"Ve hof vays of makink you talk"

I'm a little conflicted about whether my thoughts on stress interviews belong here or in the section on the dreaded idiot interviewer. Let's deal with it now. Because so much is potentially at stake, every interview is stressful to some degree. That's why I spent so much time earlier in this book showing how to control your interview anxiety. A typical interview with the typical amount of jitters is not what we're talking about here. By "stress interview" I mean one that is conducted in an impersonal, brusque, or hostile manner that is meant to intimidate you and throw you off of your prepared interview plan. The rationale (and I use the word "rationale" loosely here) for the stress interview is that the position you are applying for can be quite stressful, so they want to see how you deal with stress. This is the kind of idiocy you hear from people who don't even have a nodding acquaintance with logic or who flunked Psych 101. A stress interview doesn't measure how one deals with on-the-job stress; it demonstrates how you deal with stress interviews—that's it. They are two totally different things.

Stress interviews are opportunities for small, insecure people to inflict their latent insecurities and barely contained aggression on others whom they see as having less power. This is a human flaw that's as old as the needlessly brutal prison guard and as current as the college fraternity hazing deaths we see every year. The only two cases I can think of in which a stress interview would be a useful predictor of on-the-job performance would be if you were seeking a job as a PR person who had to tell the media why your employer was dumping cancer-causing chemicals in the drinking water, or you were applying for a legal position in which you had to defend an executive who squandered stockholder's money on stuff such as $6,000 shower curtains or ice statues that tinkle vodka. And you don't really want those jobs, do you?

Because you might run into a stress interview, you need to recognize and start dealing with it right off the bat. Early signs of a stress interview include an interviewer who doesn't make eye contact, doesn't engage in any initial pleasantries, doesn't ask you to be seated, doesn't shake hands, or starts with a rude remark such as, "Okay, let's get this done." Stay cool, stay focused, and stay courteous, because this will thwart her goal of throwing you off balance. Ask yourself what really gets under the skin of that driver who just cut you off: flipping him off or a jovial laugh and wave?

The questioning may become increasingly negative or hostile. As I discussed earlier, never let them put negative words in your mouth. If asked a question such as, "Well, if your current company is so great, why are you bailing out?" Don't be afraid to reframe the question in your answer. Try something such as, "You're right. I'm lucky to have been associated with Acme Anvil Corp., but I've learned as much as I can there, and now I'm hoping that Coyote Rocket Sleds, Inc. can offer me some new challenges." If one of your answers is rudely contradicted, don't be shy about saying something such as, "Well, I guess reasonable people can disagree," or, "I guess we can agree to disagree about that one." Always deliver these responses with a friendly smile.

If the rude behavior reaches a point at which you must say something, here's what I advise. Make a friendly but quizzical expression and say, "Excuse me, but is this one of those stress interviews? I saw them mentioned in a book by career psychologist Dr. Paul Powers, but I've never seen one before." This will throw her off balance and perhaps she'll decide to knock off the BS. If she asks you what I said about stress interviews, just laugh and say, "You don't want to know," or, "How 'bout

I tell you that after I'm hired." As you may have learned in middle school, often all it takes is a little push-back to back a bully off.

The Trained-Bear Interview

This is the interview in which you are asked to perform. This could involve role-playing a sales call, answering an angry customer's phone call, or responding to an e-mail or memo that just (hypothetically) arrived. As long as these exercises are within the area of your expertise, they represent a great opportunity to display your skills. Afterward, express your interest in the exercise and ask why that particular example was chosen and how the interviewer thought you might have handled it differently. That way, regardless of how you actually did, you are demonstrating your interest in the problems of the organization as well as showing your willingness to take feedback.

When these trained-bear interviews can be abusive is when employers use the interview process to troll for new ideas that they may use with or without you. Ad agencies sometimes ask an applicant to outline a potential campaign for a specific new client. Consulting firms may ask for a project proposal. I have seen marketers asked to submit two or three concepts for a forthcoming product launch. Graphic designers are often asked to design something "on spec" that the firm will turn around and try to sell. Although assessing your skills as accurately as possible is perfectly acceptable, pilfering your ideas for profit is not. Some companies are well known for this, and your contact network should be able to help you identify them.

If you find yourself in such a situation, you have to decide two things: do you really want to work there, and, if so, are you willing to risk their ripping you off? If the answer to both is yes, go ahead and submit your ideas, all clearly labeled in small print with "Copyright © [year] by [your name]. All rights reserved." For more details, visit the U.S. Copyright Office online at *www.copyright.gov.* This may give them pause before they rip you off. It also protects your rights if, later, you see your ideas or work in a magazine or on TV and decide to do something about it. If someone, upon seeing your copyright, has the audacity to ask, "Don't you trust us?" just brush it off with a casual, "It's just standard business practice."

Behind the Potted Palm

Job interviews can take place in such diverse locations as hotel lobbies, restaurants, airline lounges, or convention hospitality suites. The biggest problem with these settings is the excess audio and visual stimulation. This makes concentration difficult and can impinge on your ability to completely observe or hear your interviewer. Also, because some of these settings are ones in which you might tend to relax, you may let your guard down and treat the meeting with less formality than it deserves. In any of these settings, do your best to establish appropriate eye contact and do not hesitate to ask your interviewer to repeat a question if you are not sure you heard it completely. There's nothing as confusing or frustrating as giving a great response to the wrong question.

An interview outside of the interviewer's office is usually a good sign that he is trying to fit you into a busy schedule. On the other hand, a lot of executive recruiters are road warriors of the first degree, and hotel lobbies or airline lounges are de rigueur interview locations. Meals can be tricky, but are easily handled with a few simple rules. No finger food (ribs, corn on the cob, raw shellfish), nothing messy (salads, cereal, runny eggs), no booze (sorry), no sending food back, and no ogling or verbal abuse of the wait staff. Order something similar to what your interviewer orders unless it's from one of the categories mentioned here. Don't gesture with your cutlery as if you were a knife thrower from the circus. Oh, and keep in mind all that other stuff your mother told you— keep your elbows off the table, don't talk with food in your mouth, and no making a party hat with your napkin.

Seriously, though, if you feel uncertain about social graces, there are plenty of etiquette books in the library, but don't obsess about it. This isn't *Downton Abbey*, after all. All the formality you'll need is to work your way from outside to inside with the cutlery and make an X with your knife and fork (tines up) on your plate if you're still eating or parallel park them (tines down) at the 4 or 5 o'clock position if you're done.

I always get a ton of questions about drinking at a dinner interview, so I might as well go into a bit more detail. Don't. It dulls the mind, it slows your responses, and it makes you think you can sing. Despite the relaxing setting, you are not there to have fun; you are there to land a job. If pressed, you can say that you'll be driving later. If it's clear that you won't be driving later, you can say that you have some work to do or some e-mails you need to deal with later. If an idiot interviewer with a marked lack of couth has the nerve to ask if you have a problem with alcohol, avoid the temptation to give a snide reply and instead say, "No, I just prefer not to when working." This response works great and is quite useful if you are a teetotaler or are in recovery.

Trick Questions

There are a few types of trick questions you should know how to handle. Some are asked quite innocently, while others are asked with a definite agenda in mind. One not-so-innocent question concerns proprietary information you may have learned in your most recent job. If asked something along these lines, you can always say something such as, "Though I have a solid working knowledge of all areas I was involved with, I certainly wouldn't want to put you, this company, or me in hot water over a proprietary issue." This displays your sense of business ethics and alerts the interviewer that pursuing this line of questioning puts everyone at risk.

Yin or Yang

Another trick question is the forced-choice question, one that is asked in such a way that you can choose between only two answers. A couple of examples are: "Are you more of a small-company or large-company person?" and, "Are you more comfortable as a leader or as a follower?" The best way to handle this type of question is to be aware of the requirements of the job for which you are interviewing and tilt your answer in that direction. It never hurts to expand your answer a little and mention that you also see value in the option you didn't choose. You might say something such as, "Actually, I see myself as more of a leader because I like to take responsibility for making things happen. But the reality is that every boss has a boss all the way up to the president, who answers to the shareholders, so I know it pays to be a good team player as well as a team leader." Or the reverse: "Frankly, at this stage of my career the reality is that I'm more of an individual contributor, and I realize that. But I've learned a lot from working for a couple of strong leaders and that's where I'm hoping my career will go."

What If?

Hypothetical questions are easy to ask and hard to answer. These are the "What would you do if...?" questions. You hear reporters ask political candidates a lot of them. They make the interviewer seem insightful and give candidates plenty of rope with which to hang themselves. They're entertaining to watch on TV, but not especially good news for the job hunter. The only easy hypothetical questions are ones about ethics. (It goes without saying that you always take the high road on questions about ethics.) The big problem with hypotheticals is that usually not enough facts or background are given to help you put a really cogent answer together. Thus, you're sort of taking a shot in the dark.

The savvy job interviewee can put this to work in her favor by spinning out a couple of brief but (and this is important) different answers to a hypothetical question, and then add, "Of course, these are only a couple of ideas—there are multiple ways to go. Given all the variables in this situation that I don't know about, there are probably some other, perhaps better, options. I guess that's where I'd really start—getting all the data first, before deciding on a course of action." Another reason to hedge your response to a hypothetical question is that it might concern an internal issue that your prospective employer is facing at that very moment. If you come down on the wrong side of it, you could be doing yourself some damage.

From Way out in Left Field

We've all heard stories about interviewers who ask inane questions. Although the category is endless, the following are a few actual interview questions job hunters have shared with me. Enjoy.

"If you could be a tree (or animal), what type would you be?"

"Do you believe in UFOs?"

"What weighs more—a ton of iron or a ton of feathers?"

"Do you read your horoscope?"

No matter how stupid a question seems, I heartily suggest that you stifle your urge to break out laughing at your interviewer. (Save that for happy hour with your pals.) Your interviewer may have asked the question as an icebreaker. He may have asked the question because somebody asked it of him years ago and he thought it was cool. He may have asked it out of nervousness. He may have asked it because he couldn't think of anything else to ask. Or he may have asked it to see how you deal with inane situations. Who knows?

My suggestion is to tread carefully, say nothing provocative, and play it safe with a generic answer. Even if you genuinely believe in little green men or have always secretly wanted to be a badger, I'd keep these thoughts to yourself. If you get hired, they'll find out soon enough just how weird you really are. No sense rushing things.

The Dreaded Idiot Interviewer

Asking an occasional inane question does not automatically qualify someone as the dreaded idiot interviewer. Repeatedly asking stupid questions will, however, do the trick. Asking overly personal questions or asking questions of an overtly political or religious nature certainly qualify. And asking clearly illegal questions is the hallmark of the dreaded idiot interviewer.

Dr. Paul's Law of the Distribution of Jerks and Idiots says, "Jerks and idiots are distributed more or less evenly throughout society." This is good news; otherwise, we would probably have entire towns or companies composed only of jerks and idiots. Having a few jerks here and a couple of idiots over there dilutes the negative effect these clueless folks have on the rest of us. It gives us hope that society won't end up looking like the guest panel on *Jerry Springer*. But it also means that every now and then you will run into a jerk or an idiot, and this includes your job interviewers.

It's hard to be a great job candidate when the person asking the questions is a loser, but it can be done. Early on in this book you learned that if you take the advice and counsel I have offered, you will probably be much more skilled in interviewing than the person who is interviewing you. Sometimes, well-intentioned but unskilled people make mistakes. Keeping this in mind will prevent you from jumping down the throat of the interviewer at the sound of the first idiotic or potentially illegal question.

If you hear a question that strikes you as inappropriate, there are a couple of approaches you can try. I suggest that you first consider how a bluntly honest answer might affect your candidacy; if you see no problem, answer it. Otherwise, try to redirect the question into fair territory. If you are asked if you are married or dating or plan to have children, you might respond with, "I keep my work life and personal life separate. I have no problem with the time investment required for this job or the travel that we discussed, if that's what you're asking." The interviewer may have had that perfectly acceptable concern but didn't know how to ask the question in a legal manner. An illegally phrased question about religion might be masking legitimate issues of your availability to work certain hours or days. A question about national origin or citizenship might be a bobbled attempt at compliance with changing immigration laws or security clearance regulations. By giving the interviewer the benefit of the doubt, you may be able to prevent his interviewing incompetence from preventing you from getting a job that you really want. Keeping a cool head and responding in a civil, forthright manner while helping an interviewer out of a hole he inadvertently dug for himself can win you many points.

If you continue to get questions that make you uncomfortable (two is my limit, but you might have a bit more tolerance than I do), it is time for another, more assertive approach. You might respond with, "Mr. Burns, I'm very interested in this position because I think it's a great fit between what you need and what I have to offer. I want to remove any doubt about this that you have, but, frankly, I don't see the relevance of that question to this position." This is a clearly confrontational response, but I suggest you keep the tone professional and assertive without crossing the line into personal and aggressive. Your goal in this (and in every) interview is to generate a job offer, even if you ultimately reject it or use it only to help you generate other offers. I am not suggesting that you submit to a single iota of abuse or illegal discrimination; at all times you retain the ultimate power of terminating the interview and leaving.

If you do walk out or feel afterward that your rights were violated, what do you do? Complain to the authorities, write a letter to the editor, inform your network, or file a lawsuit? This is a very personal decision and I can't make it for you. As your career coach—someone who is 100-percent focused on your career success—I'd have to say walk away and find a better job in a better organization with a better boss. Don't get mad, and don't waste your valuable time trying to get even. My advice: *get ahead*. Living well is the best revenge, my friend.

But that advice is coming from a guy who never saw a N.I.N.A (No Irish Need Apply) sign in a Boston shop window, who was never shunted to a separate water fountain or restroom, who hasn't sat at the curb in a wheelchair trying to figure out how to get to a third-floor interview, and who has never worried that his accent labels him as a potential terrorist. After leaving an interview in which you think (not just feel) that you were asked illegal questions, you must first determine if those potentially unlawful questions were asked for the purpose of discriminating against you because of an illegal reason or had the net effect of discriminating against you.

As an interviewer becomes more interested in hiring you, it is natural for her to want to know more about you as a person. (Refer back to Figure 4.2 in Chapter 4.) This helps the interviewer to "make a clear distinction" (the first definition of the word discriminate) between you and other candidates. If an interviewer asks a stupid or illegal question—say, about your having children—but the employer has an exemplary record for hiring and accommodating working parents, then any legal action you take will most likely be fruitless, time consuming, and stressful, and won't do your career any good. The nub of the legal issue is that though it is clearly stupid to ask illegal questions, it is not necessarily illegal to ask stupid questions.

If you feel that it is your duty to raise questions about potential illegal discrimination, contact your state employment or equal opportunity agency and the federal EEOC (Equal Employment Opportunity Commission) simultaneously. Typically, the Feds defer to the state agency to make the preliminary inquiries, and your filing needs to be within 180 days (by which date I hope you are gainfully employed). These agencies are woefully underfunded and have a huge backlog of cases; I have seen some of these cases go on for years. Even if nothing comes of your complaint, you may be called to offer testimony at a later date, when an even more egregious violation comes to light.

The legal route is a tough road to go, but you may decide that you have no choice but to pursue it. One former job hunter calling in to my radio show talked about facing this choice. He was insulted enough that he couldn't drop the issue, but he was wary about risking his career options, upon which his extended family depended. He created a third path forward by harnessing his psychic energy regarding this issue by helping to establish a mentoring and tutoring program for kids in his church from single-parent homes. He didn't merely get mad, he didn't try to get even, he helped others to get ahead, and, as a bonus, he felt better about himself. As another option, maybe something like this would work for you.

Possible Interview Calamities

I say possible calamities because most problems that arise in an interview can be fixed. It takes a little work and you have to stay cool, but issues can usually be resolved. For example, sometimes miscommunication happens. If you mistakenly arrive an hour early for an interview, you can always excuse yourself and go for a walk. This is much better than sitting and waiting in the lobby because you can dissipate your nervous energy. If (gulp) you mistakenly arrive an hour late for an interview, apologize profusely (regardless of whose fault it was), say how much you were looking forward to the meeting, and offer to reschedule at their convenience. On the few occasions I've heard of this happening, they have just gone ahead with the interview.

Resume Errors

I've already cautioned you about having any inaccuracies on your resume—at some point they will be discovered. These errors cast doubt on everything else on your resume and raise questions about your truthfulness in general. But we're all human, and mistakes happen. A minor error such as a date that is off by a year is not the same as listing an academic degree you never received or an employer for whom you never worked. The former you can pass off as a typo (still an issue on this important document), but the latter is a deal-breaker. You can try to hem and haw, but if you included this data on purpose, you've done it more than once and you won't be able to blame it on some grievous secretarial error. Accept that you've been found out and exit as gracefully as you can, sadder but wiser.

Fuhgeddaboutit

No matter how you try to control your interview stress, some of it is going to creep in. If it contributes to keeping you alert and on your toes, that's great. But sometimes it can get in the way of remembering some of your best-prepared responses or your most telling anecdotes or your most insightful questions. This is the sort of brain freeze that happens when someone makes a snide remark to you and a killer comeback doesn't come to you until later that evening. During the ride home after every interview, there will be a moment when you make a fist, tap it on your forehead, and say, "Ooh, why didn't I say...?" Or, even worse, you say, "What was I thinking when I said...?"

There is an easy way to fix either of these problems: the thank-you/follow-up note. It should look professional (typed, spell-checked, printed on good paper if sending hard copy), use the correct spelling of the person's name and correct title (check this with the business card you asked for), and should be sent immediately after the interview. Along with your new or revised comments, you should reiterate your appreciation for the interview and strong interest in the job. Although particularly helpful in the situations described in the previous sections, this is something you should do after every interview. It's just one more way of communicating, "I'm thorough, I'm really interested, and I'm courteous." It's like getting one more chance at bat after the inning is over.

Dem Rattlin' Bones

All of us have an episode that we hope won't show up when they make the made-for-TV movie of our life. It may be as unimportant as a lampshade on your head at the office party; it may be as personal as an ugly divorce; it may be as serious as a bankruptcy; or it may be as germane as being fired from your last job. It could be something silly or stupid that was once on a social networking site. Ask yourself, "What is it I really hope I will never get asked about in a job interview?" Write that question down and then prepare an emotionally neutral, factually accurate response that doesn't dwell on the event or delve too far into it. If there is a skeleton rattling away anywhere in your closet, sometime, somewhere, a skilled, insightful interviewer will dig it up. It's nothing to lose sleep about as long as you have adequately prepared for it.

You Want to Know What?!

Some organizations do not rely solely on interviews and references to evaluate job candidates. Many use various testing methods. Some are useful, some are not, but you should know what to expect if you run into them.

Drug Tests

It is now quite common to find the question, "Do you consent to take a drug test as a condition of employment?" on company application forms. If you check no (and it is noticed), you will probably no longer be in the running for the job in question. You and I may debate the ethics, legality, and appropriateness of this fact, but we need to intelligently face this modern reality. If you check yes, sometimes this is the last you ever hear of it. However, most of the time you can expect to be asked to supply a urine sample for testing after you have accepted the job offer but before you actually start your new job.

I wish I could say "Just don't do drugs and you'll have nothing to worry about," but I can't. The problem is the unacceptable rate of "false positive" results that these tests produce. A "false positive" result is one that shows a non-drug-using test subject as a drug user. The estimated rate of false positives range between 5 percent (in tightly controlled research settings) to more than 50 percent! There are a number of reasons for this. Some pastries and bagels contain poppy seeds that may show up as morphine. Many common over-the-counter medications contain ibuprofen, which may have you test positive for marijuana. Some popular nighttime cough and cold medications may have you test positive for opiates. And, naturally, any medications legally prescribed by your physician for a range of conditions can be expected to show up, as well. And we haven't even touched on the issues of unregulated testing labs, poorly supervised testing protocols, or minimum-wage lab workers holding your professional reputation in their minimally trained (and possibly drug-tainted) hands. And yet more companies, government agencies, and unions are mandating these tests. So what are you to do?

First of all, for all the reasons we know so well, don't do illegal drugs. If you are faced with a drug test, here is your strategy. State that you don't use illegal drugs and that you don't object to the test per se. But add that you have read about the alarmingly high rate of false positives that they generate. Then ask a few questions:

➤ Is this testing program run by a physician (sometimes called an MRO or medical review officer)? A competent, well-trained medical person is apt to handle the test more professionally than somebody fresh from the muffler shop.

➤ Does this testing program use only federally certified testing labs?

➤ In the event of a false positive, do I have the right to a retest?

➤ Are the results sent elsewhere or are they retained with complete confidentiality?

If you are given a form to fill out asking about which medications you have taken ("recently" or "within the last week"), go back three weeks (because some compounds stay in your body that long) and list every prescription, every over-the-counter medicine, and every nutritional supplement you may have used during that time. Oh, and double-check to make sure that your, ahem, "sample" is accurately labeled so it won't be confused with the one from the guy with the dancing bear tattoo.

We all have a right to a drug-free workplace, and if you doubt this, consider how you'd feel, wondering if the pilot of your next airplane trip or the driver of the huge dump truck next to you on the freeway or the doctor delivering your baby or the cop on the street corner is high. Drug-testing programs are here to stay and will continue to improve in quality and reliability. Who knows? One day companies and the government may even choose to address alcohol abuse at work, which is estimated to cost 10 times more than drugs in terms of accidents and lost productivity.

Psychological Tests

Many organizations conduct psychological assessments of the leading candidates for key positions. Done professionally, this is a moderately expensive process, so the good news is that if you are asked to complete a battery of assessment tools, you have definitely made the short list of candidates. On the other hand, there is a fair share of useless so-called assessment tools, and many "consultants" out there selling assessment services with minimal or no psychological training. At best, a well-conducted assessment can closely determine the degree of fit between you, the job, and the hiring organization. At worst, it can be no more effective than someone trying to read the bumps on your head. In any event, it is another hurdle for you to jump before landing the job for which you have been working so hard for.

As with drug testing, I suggest you express your willingness to participate, and then follow up with a few informed questions:

➤➤ Is the person conducting the assessment a licensed psychologist or psychiatrist? Other "testers" may or may not have adequate training and access to the best tools, and are not bound by rigid ethical and professional guidelines.

➤➤ Does he have an extensive background in employment and human resources? Many great shrinks out there have little knowledge of the world of work. A licensed psychologist with experience in this area will use only assessment tools that are statistically reliable and valid, and that are appropriate for the situation.

➥ Will the person conducting the assessment explain the tools to you or do you have to take them "blind"? There is no secret voodoo to bona fide assessment tests, and there is no reason why a competent professional wouldn't provide a full explanation.

➥ Are these tests being used as a thumbs-up or thumbs-down on your selection? Psychological testing is best used as part of a three-part assessment process that also includes the results of personal interviews and data gathered from job references.

➥ Whether or not you are hired, will the person who conducted the assessment share the results with you? Some will; others will not. If asked, I share the information with an unsuccessful candidate because I feel it can help the person as he continues with his job search. If the person is hired, I try to arrange a meeting with the new boss and the candidate to use the data to facilitate the assimilation process.

I've been asked if you can or should try to "fool" these tests. Generally speaking, I'd say no. Although you can slant your responses somewhat, the best tools have internal measures for inconsistency, guessing, or faking. Further, I'd have to ask you why you would want a job you weren't really suitedfor . That said, I do have a success strategy for you to use when asked to take a psychological assessment battery.

Before you take the tests, do this exercise. Close your eyes and think of the best couple of days you have ever had at work. Now open your eyes and make a list of words (nouns, verbs, adjectives, it doesn't matter) that describes you on those occasions. Do this a couple of times. Close your eyes again. Picture in your mind's eye a day sometime in the future when you are really succeeding at the job for which you are testing. Open your eyes and add to your self-descriptive list.

Now you have a comprehensive list of the qualities and traits to emphasize in the testing. You are not being asked to reveal every little thing about every aspect of your life. You are being assessed for personality and certain work behaviors such as leadership, independence, and decision-making style. You are a person of many colors, but only certain ones come out at work (or come out most frequently at work), and your best colors shine through on your best days. By keeping your best days in mind, your "true colors come shining through."

Integrity Testing

If I haven't stirred up a hornet's nest yet, this next section should do the trick. It's a fact that American industry loses tens of billions of dollars a year from employee theft. I saw one article that suggested the number might be as high as $50 billion, and it didn't take into account the growing spate of executive piracy, which is rarely punished. It's natural that employers would want to address this issue on the hiring side of the problem at the same time they address it with stronger monitoring of current employees. This has given rise to the whole (lucrative) area of honesty or integrity testing, which has about as much usefulness as the old test for witches. The accused witch was bound hand and foot and thrown in the river. If she floated, she was a witch. If she didn't float, she wasn't a witch. Either way, this poor lady had a really bad day because the likelihood was that if she didn't die by hanging or burning, she would probably die by drowning. The key, it seems, was the same one I devised long ago for high school chemistry: try to get out of taking the test if humanly possible. The same goes for integrity testing.

Hook Me Up, Baby

Let's take the most famous test in this category—the polygraph, also known as the lie detector. This is a machine that detects changes in such physiological reactions as blood pressure, heartbeat, and respiration. The research is mixed on whether these changes, in fact, indicate whether a person is lying. In folks who are basically honest, it shows physical discomfort with some questions. But a pathological or practiced liar can beat the machine repeatedly. Many years ago, Congress passed legislation banning the use of these machines in most employment settings. As the government is prone to do, it exempted itself (and certain outside contractors) from this regulation protecting employee rights. If you apply for a defense department, FBI, CIA, DEA, NSA, ATF, TSA, or homeland security position, you may well be asked to take a polygraph test. Before the test, practice your deep breathing and relaxation techniques, and try to continue to use them during it. It may help your performance on the test, and at the very least, it will help reduce your stress during it. I would be remiss if I didn't mention that the traitors in some of the biggest U.S. spy cases never had a problem passing their polygraph tests. I guess that's one of the upsides of being a sociopath.

A Mini-Intelligence Test

More and more companies are turning to paper-and-pencil honesty testing despite the minor problem that it doesn't work. Okay, I guess it sometimes works if a job candidate actually admits he's a lying, thieving bastard (interesting interview strategy there, eh?). But private and government studies show that thousands of honest applicants get screened out (rejected) to find the very few dishonest ones. One study showed that more than 90 percent of applicants labeled dishonest or potentially dishonest were inaccurately assessed. As a Diplomate of the American Board of Psychological Specialties and the American College of Forensic Examiners, I eagerly anticipate a class-action lawsuit on this front.

This is why I suggest you view these types of tests as mini-intelligence tests. First, it measures and demonstrates how uninformed (or lazy) your potential employer's hiring practices are. You need to determine if this means that there is a lot of room for the improvements you can bring to this employer or whether they are so out to lunch that you want to avoid them completely.

On the other hand, this mini-intelligence test applies to you, too. If you take such a test, you will see questions asking if you "ever" felt guilty or "ever" told a lie, or asking for a true-or-false response to the statement that you "never" took an employer's office supplies. Be wary of questions with absolute words such as *ever* and *never*, because if you try to paint a picture of perfect sainthood, you will be labeled as attempting to fake your responses. Most of these tests are not timed, so before you start, scan it to see if you can find repeated or very similar questions so that you respond to them consistently. Your best strategy is to review the list of positive self-descriptions you compiled to deal with the psych tests. Keep this professional, positive, but realistic image foremost in your mind and you will do fine.

Oh, and just to make you feel a little better about this stuff, drug tests, polygraph tests, and these so-called honesty tests are rarely given to those occupying the executive suite.

Your Best Problem Ever

You've worked hard, found a great opportunity, interviewed like a champ, got the job offer, negotiated it upward a bit, accepted it, and settled on a start date. Then, the unimaginable happens. You get another offer. I have seen this happen only a few times with the folks I've advised, because they usually follow my recommendation to conduct a sweep for other potential offers when they get the first one in hand. But it happens.

If the job isn't a better fit with your goals, or the compensation package is far off target, your decision is easy. But if it's a better job with more compensation, your decision is tougher. Loyalty is a two-way street, and you owe an employer only the loyalty you feel you will get in return. Today's organizational reality is that if your employer's fortunes head downward, you could be gone before the next pay period. So, if you get a better job offer and you have done the analysis to prove it is better and you have not yet started your new job, I'd say take the better offer. If the offer is roughly equivalent, I'd say reject the new offer. If the offer is better but you've already started your new job, only take it if it is *substantially* better because, at some point, you will have to deal with the negative fallout for having bailed out on an employer and team that was counting on you.

It never ceases to amaze me how entire industries, professions, and multinational corporations are like small towns. Even people who don't know you personally have heard of you or know someone who knows you. After all, that's what networking is all about. As in all areas of job hunting, be careful about burning any bridges, because, as the Little Feat song says, "The same people you misuse on your way up, you might meet 'em on the way down."

Chapter 10

Getting From Good to Great

IF YOU HAVE READ THIS BOOK FROM THE BEGINNING AND ONLY PICKED UP ON HALF OF WHAT I HAVE SHARED, you could probably walk into an interview right now and do a pretty good job. It might be one of your best interviews ever. But this is a potentially dangerous trap.

By now you may have already realized that the competition out there is smarter and tougher than the last time you were job hunting. Add to this fact whatever family financial reality you may be facing during this job hunt. And just to make things a bit more exciting, let's hypothesize that the unpredictable ups and downs we are observing in today's employment world will continue well into the future.

What all this means is that in today's job market, a *good* interviewing performance may not be *good enough* to land you the job you want. If you are a serious job hunter and you want to land a good job in less time, with less stress, and get paid more to do it, then you have got to ratchet up your interviewing skills from *good* to *great*.

I do not say this to scare you. I emphasize it because I want you to be well-informed and forearmed. I've already done the informing and now I'm going to do the arming.

For this chapter I have constructed a number of tools to help you ramp up your interviewing skills from good to great. There are quizzes, checklists, sample forms, typical questions, informational pieces, and practice guidelines. Some you will use only once (per job hunt) and others you will need to use time and again. Feel free to make photocopies of the ones you want to use more than once.

I have referenced these tools in earlier chapters of this book. However, they are all stand-alone tools that you can peruse at your convenience. There is one minor problem with these tools: they are not going to jump out of this book and go to work for you while you're snoozing on the couch. You must pull the tools out and put them to work on your behalf. Add to them, modify them, and bend them to your purpose. The only mistake you can make is ignoring them. Remember, what was once good enough may not be good enough today. If you are serious about this process and want to be a great job interviewer, here is how you do it. You work at it. You out-prepare the competition. You use every tool at your disposal.

I'd like to emphasize one more time that great job candidates are created, not born. *It is within your power* to get more and better interviews, to knock your interviewers' socks off when you get in front of them, to have glowing references, and to generate and then successfully negotiate better job offers than you ever thought possible. I have shown you how to do it. All it takes from you is focus and effort. Landing a job that lights you up, finding a job you love, and building a career that helps you become your best self is within your grasp. Will you reach out and take it?

The Good to Great Interview Toolkit

Tool #1: Job-Hunt Readiness Assessment

Directions: Answer the following questions by circling yes or no.

1. Can I describe my current target in one or two
    concise sentences?   Yes   No
2. Can I describe myself (your elevator pitch) in
    one or two concise sentences?   Yes   No

3. Am I willing to make my job hunt a priority by investing enough time and energy to make it successful?   Yes   No

4. Have I had a heart-to-heart talk with those closest to me about the support I'll need during this process?   Yes   No

5. Is my resume up to date?   Yes   No

6. Have I reviewed my social media profile and tuned it up appropriately?   Yes   No

7. Have I practiced my interviewing skills, preferably with videotaped role playing?   Yes   No

8. Have I identified multiple sources of published job openings?   Yes   No

9. Have I compiled a preliminary list of my networking contacts?   Yes   No

10. Have I identified a list of appropriate employment recruiters who know my geographic target area, my functional specialty, and my industry?   Yes   No

11. Have I learned how to use the Internet to uncover job listings?   Yes   No

12. Have I asked my reference librarian what job-hunting resources are available at my local and regional libraries?   Yes   No

13. Do I know where to find the salary ranges of the jobs I'm considering?   Yes   No

14. Do I have a quiet, private place from which to make phone calls and get voice mail?   Yes   No

15. Have I contacted my job references and prepared them to speak on my behalf?   Yes   No

16. Do I have two or three favorite interview outfits put aside in which I both look good and feel good?   Yes   No

17. Do I have a system set up to keep track of my job-hunting expenses so I can deduct them on my income tax return?   Yes   No

18. Have I tuned up or updated the electronic tools
I'll need in the process?   Yes   No

19. Have I identified a job-search support group to
join to help me keep my spirits up during
this process?   Yes   No

20. Have I set up an exercise schedule to help me
maintain my energy level and positive attitude
during this process?   Yes   No

Scoring:

a.   If you answered yes to all 20 questions, you are well prepared
to start a successful job hunt. Congratulations.

b.   If you answered no to between one to three questions, you
are in good shape but you probably need to do a little more
work on the foundation of your job hunt. Do it now.

c.   If you answered no to more than three questions, you are not
ready to start your job hunt and you could make some critical
mistakes that will hurt you in the long run. Read this entire
book and all the tools in this toolkit to help you find what you
need. Remember, nobody was born great at this, but with my
support you can go from merely good to great!

Tool #2: Controlling Interview Anxiety

Anxiety is a normal human reaction and is experienced by every
human being at some point. It is natural to be nervous or uneasy before
an interview. This happens to even the most experienced job candidates.
Using the ideas and techniques found in Chapter 2, the vast majority of
job hunters can not only control their interview anxiety, but also harness
it to improve their interviewing performance.

There is, however, a significant difference between everyday anxiety
and an anxiety *disorder*. There are a few different types of anxiety disor-
ders, including generalized anxiety disorder, panic disorder, social anxiety disorder, and specific phobias. These are serious issues wherein fear
and worry can be constant, crippling, and negatively affect all aspects of
your life, not just job interviewing. I have had job candidates describe to
me every one of the following reactions at one time or other.

If you *regularly* experience two or three of the following emotional, physical, or cognitive symptoms, you should consult with a licensed

mental health professional. Psychologists, psychiatrists, and licensed clinical social workers trained in this area have a host of therapeutic approaches (including cognitive behavioral therapy sometimes combined with medication) that can help you successfully address these issues. Please do not let pride or needless embarrassment prevent you from enjoying the life and career you deserve.

Cognitive Reactions

➤ Thinking something bad is going to happen
➤ Self-consciousness
➤ Flashbacks
➤ Inability to control images
➤ Heartbeat seems louder
➤ Irrational thoughts
➤ Distorted sense of time elapsed
➤ Inability to control thoughts
➤ Obsessive thoughts
➤ Negative thoughts
➤ Fearful images
➤ Rushing
➤ Memory loss
➤ Sensory deprivation
➤ Avoidance of people
➤ Freezing
➤ Difficulty concentrating
➤ Racing thoughts

Emotional Reactions

➤ Fear that the anxiety will take over
➤ Absence of emotional affect/flatness
➤ Feeing at physical risk
➤ Disconnectedness
➤ Moodiness (anger/sadness)

➤ Aggressive responses
➤ Nightmares

Physical Reactions

➤ Sweaty palms
➤ Cold/clammy palms
➤ Racing or pounding heartbeat
➤ Excessive blushing
➤ Shortness of breath or hyperventilation
➤ Dry throat, dry mouth, and thick tongue
➤ Dizziness
➤ Headaches
➤ Distorted/tunnel vision
➤ Distorted hearing
➤ Nausea/queasiness
➤ Constipation or diarrhea
➤ Poor motor control
➤ Muscle tension or stiffness
➤ Shaking legs
➤ Wobbly knees
➤ Trembling hands
➤ Stumbling
➤ Heavy legs
➤ Frozen movements
➤ Poor balance
➤ Insomnia
➤ Voice cracks
➤ Voice constricts and pitch increases
➤ Shaking voice
➤ Suddenly feeling hot or cold (for no reason)
➤ Cold feet

Tool #3: Tax Tips for the Job Hunter

When hunting for a job in your given profession, there are some out-of-pocket expenses that you should be able to deduct on your Federal income tax return. Nothing is simple when dealing with tax returns, however, and there are ifs, buts, and maybes you need to look at. Most of all, be sure to a) save all your receipts and b) consult with a CPA before taking any tax deductions.

If you are searching for a job in a new trade or business, your job search expenses are not tax deductible. Naturally, new trade or business is not clearly defined. If a plumber becomes a lawyer, that is a new trade or business. If a taxi driver becomes a bus driver, that would not sound like a new trade or business. Under this concept, a person searching for her first job or one after an extended time out of work might not qualify for deducting her job search expenses.

Items that are deductible:

» Resume printing.

» Stationery and mailing of resumes and follow-up correspondence.

» Long-distance telephone calls with prospective employers.

» Your Internet service.

» Travel and transportation expenses for interviews or search for employment including air fare, train fare, taxis, parking, tolls, overnight travel, meals while traveling, or automobile expenses (go online to research the current IRS standard rate per mile).

» Fees to career consultants.

» Cost of publications containing potential job openings.

You'll be surprised how the cost of the previous items can mount up, so don't be shy about taking these legitimate deductions.

In order to claim these items, taxpayers must itemize their deductions. Job-search expenses fall into the miscellaneous category of deductions, which means that when combined with other miscellaneous itemized deductions, they are only deductible to the extent that they exceed 2 percent of adjusted gross income (AGI). In addition, these expenses might provide no benefit if you are subject to the alternative minimum tax (AMT). See? This is why I told you to consult a CPA.

Items that are not deductible:

➤➤ Clothing for interviews.

➤➤ Haircuts and other personal grooming items for interviews.

➤➤ Travel to locations whereby the travel is primarily personal pleasure in nature. (There goes that interview trip to Tahiti.)

I compiled the previous information with the invaluable assistance of John M. Hoffman and Associates, Certified Public Accountants, with offices in Boston, Massachusetts and Savannah, Georgia (*www.hoffman.com*).

Any mistakes, however, are mine so for the third time I'll tell you to get some professional help with your taxes.

Tool #4: Job Hunt Goal-Setting and Monitoring

Goals for week (or month) of:

Obviously, you won't be engaging in every one of these job-search activities every week. Adjust your goals to the appropriate stage of your job hunt. Don't gloss over this tool. Setting clear goals and honestly measuring your progress toward them will help you refine and customize your plan with up-to-the-minute results and feedback. This is essential for you to go from good to great in this process.

Part I

	Projected	Actual
1. My current job target(s).		
2. Hours to invest in job hunt.		
3. Hours to find and respond to published openings.		
4. Hours to research potential employers and do targeted mailing.		

5. Hours to identify and contact agencies, recruiters, and search consultants.		
6. Hours to read job-hunting books.		
7. Hours to scan job-listing Websites.		
8. Hours to identify, contact, and expand personal network (total): a) By phone b) By e-mail c) In person d) Via social media		
9. Hours to identify and prepare job references.		
10. Hours to practice interviewing skills.		
11. Hours in actual interviews.		
12. Hours for administrative activities (filing, copying, thank-you letters).		
13. Other.		

Part II

Based on the evaluation in Part I:

What's working:	
What's not working:	
I need to increase:	
I need to decrease:	
Other feedback/changes I should make:	
My reward for accomplishing these goals:	

Tool # 5: Research Resources

After a few weeks of active job hunting, it is going to be hard for you to remember all the sources of useful information you uncovered, where you found them, who helped you find them, and where they are physically located. Whenever you find a helpful research resource, log in the relevant data. You may have to quickly find this information again as you prepare for upcoming interviews, during job-offer analysis and negotiation, or future job searches.

Helpful data:

Source of data:

How to find data:

Date found:

Library or database:

Physical location:

Name of reference librarian or contact:

Helpful data:

Source of data:

How to find data:

Date found:

Library or database:

Physical location:

Name of reference librarian or contact:

Helpful data:

Source of data:

How to find data:

Date found:

Library or database:

Physical location:

Name of reference librarian or contact:

Capture and retain in your career file all data, resources, and tools that you have found helpful during this job hunt for quicker access during your next job hunt.

Tool #6: Building Your Contact Network

I. How you build, maintain, use, and grow your network of personal contacts will have an overarching effect on your ability to generate job leads and interviews. Here are a few facts:

1. Your contact network will only expand from this moment forward.

2. It would be fantastic if any of your contacts had a bona fide job opening for you, but this is unlikely. Your goal is to gather two things from your contacts: (1) data you can use to generate job leads, and (2) access to new contacts. (See Section II.)

3. Your initial network of contacts is larger than you think. (See Section III.)

4. You will get more usable information from those farthest away from your initial list of contacts. (Remember the strength of

weak ties.) Thus, the very essence of effective networking is *expanding* your network.

5. There is no rule that says you can ask a contact for ideas and leads only once during your job search. Every couple of weeks you can "keep them posted" on your progress and tap them for new input.

II. Don't beat around the bush. Tell everyone on your initial contact list that you are starting a job search and hope you can count on their help. Assuming they say yes, tell them what you are looking for and ask the following questions:

1. Do they know of any immediate openings of the sort you are looking for? Do they have a contact name for you? Can they make an introduction?

2. What sources of published openings are they familiar with (places to find job postings, help-wanted ads, newspapers, Websites, job banks, alumni groups, association or professional newsletters, and so on)?

3. What libraries, research resources, or databases have they found helpful in their job searches?

4. What is their sense of your industry/company targets? Do they have any inside sources?

5. Do they know any employment agencies, contingency recruiters, or executive search consultants they can introduce you to?

6. Will they give you the names and numbers of four or five people they know who they think have the best or widest network that you might be able to tap into to find more of this same type of information?

Close the conversation with your thanks and let them know you'll periodically be "keeping them posted." (See Section I, Question 5.)

III. The key to thoroughly identifying your initial contact list is to ask yourself what constituencies you are a member of. The more extensive your initial contact list is, the more extensive your expanded contact network list will be, the more job leads you will generate, the more interviews you will land, the more offers you will get, and, ultimately, the shorter your job search will be. To help you build this critical first level of network contacts, list the people you know who are members of the following groups.

1. Your family (immediate and extended).
2. Your in-laws (current and former).
3. Your friends and social group.
4. Your current work colleagues/acquaintances (discretion is advised).
5. Your current customers, vendors, suppliers, and consultants.
6. Your colleagues from previous jobs.
7. Your bosses from previous jobs.
8. Customers, vendors, suppliers, and consultants from previous jobs.
9. People you've met at professional meetings, conferences, and conventions.
10. People in your technical, professional, or trade groups.
11. Your job references.
12. People with whom you have interviewed in the past.
13. Neighbors and former neighbors.
14. Personal contacts from school (yours and spouse's).
15. People you've met in the PTA.
16. Your holiday card list.
17. Members of your church, social, civic, athletic, community, and political groups.
18. Your alumni association.
19. Your personal consultants (for example, attorney, clergy, accountant, hairdresser, mechanic, dentist, insurance person, trainer).
20. Contacts from any job-search groups you join.

I've combined a number of these groups together, but you catch my drift. You know more people than you think you do. Now go to work and turn them into a network that can help you land a job you love.

Tool #7: Frequently Asked Interview Questions

As you prepare for your interviews, read each question and prepare a solid answer for it. You may not get the exact same questions in your interview, but you will get some that are quite close.

As you have read in Chapter 5, I want you to practice your interviewing skills in hour-long, videotaped mock interviews. Before you start this process, identify the questions you want your interviewer to use, but allow him or her to choose some to throw in as well.

Your personal qualities:

1. What are your greatest strengths?
2. What are your greatest weaknesses?
3. How would your colleagues describe you?
4. What types of people rub you the wrong way?
5. How do you handle conflict?
6. Tell me about yourself.
7. What is unique about you?
8. What turns you off?
9. Are you a born leader or a natural follower?
10. What motivates you?
11. Are you a better written communicator or a better verbal communicator?
12. Tell me how you handled a difficult social situation.
13. What are your hobbies and interests? What do you do in your spare time?
14. What is your energy level like?
15. How have you learned from your disappointments?
16. Do you prefer working with others or working alone?
17. Describe your personality.
18. What bores you? Why? How do you avoid it?
19. What public figure do you admire? Why?
20. What do you want out of life?

Your education:

1. How did you do in high school? What were your favorite and least favorite courses? Who were your favorite teachers? What sports and activities did you do? What offices did you hold?
2. Why did you choose the college you attended?
3. Why did you choose your course of study?
4. Did you enjoy the school? Why or why not?
5. What extracurricular activities were you involved in? Were they worth the time you put into them?
6. How much of your schooling did you pay for yourself? How?
7. Did you work while you were in school? Doing what? Did it help or hurt your grades?
8. How did your academic/training background prepare you for this job/organization?
9. If you could do your schooling over, what would you change? Why?
10. Could you have done better in school? How? Why didn't you?
11. What continuing professional training have you completed since graduating?
12. What are your future educational plans? What have you done about them?

Your career:

1. Explain your career path.
2. What was your first job? What did you learn from it? (Same question for every other job.)
3. Who was your favorite boss? Why?
4. Who was your worst boss? Why?
5. What parts of your schoolwork most prepared you for work? How?
6. What obstacles have you had to overcome to succeed?
7. Where do you see yourself in three, five, and 10 years?
8. Explain how you operate in a team environment.
9. Should people in your field be paid more?

10. What are your financial goals? Are you on track to reach them?

11. What is the difference in the way you treat subordinates vs. superiors?

12. How have you handled a disagreement with a boss and/or with a peer?

13. Have you ever been fired? Why?

14. Have you ever fired someone? How?

15. From your resume, show me a good example of teamwork.

16. From your resume, show me a good example of your work ethic and initiative.

17. Have you had any jobs that do not appear on your resume?

18. What are your greatest accomplishments?

19. Tell me about a big mistake that you made at work.

20. What types of people will you not work with?

21. How long do you want to continue working?

22. What are the disadvantages of your chosen field?

23. Do you prefer a large or small company?

24. Will you go where the company sends you?

25. Looking back over your career, what do you wish you had done differently?

26. Where do you see your career going?

This job:

1. How did you hear about this opening?

2. Why should we hire you for this job?

3. What do you bring to this job that is different from anyone else?

4. Why do you want to leave your current job/company?

5. How much are you currently making? How much do you want to make?

6. What are you looking for in your next job?

7. Evaluate your current boss for me.

8. What do you like best about your current job?

9. Why did you receive your last promotion?
10. How does this job compare with others you've applied for?
11. What are some things you and your boss have disagreed about?
12. What is it about this job that appeals to you most?
13. In what ways has your current job prepared you for this one?
14. How does this job fit in with your overall career plans?
15. What makes you think you can succeed in this job?
16. What are your short-term objectives?
17. What other organizations are you interviewing with?
18. What aspect of this job excites you the most?
19. How would you modify this position to best suit your skills?
20. May I check your references?
21. When can you start?
22. If we offer you this job, will you accept it?
23. Will you stay with your current employer if they make you a counteroffer?
24. What is your transition plan for the job you're leaving?
25. What will your current boss say/do when you tell her you're leaving?

This company:
1. What do you know about our company?
2. What attracts you to our organization?
3. What is our reputation in the marketplace?
4. What have you learned about our organizational culture?
5. Why do you think this company will be any better than your last?
6. Do you know anyone who works for us?
7. How familiar are you with our products or services?
8. What do you specifically bring to our company that it needs?
9. Have you read our annual report?
10. What research have you done about our organization?

11. Have you read any articles about us in the press?

12. Can you see spending the rest of your career with us?

General:

1. What's most important to you?

2. Are you interested in sports? Are you interested in the arts?

3. Do you do charity work? Are you involved in your community?

4. What did your parents do for work? Which one has had the biggest influence on you?

5. Do you have brothers or sisters?

6. What was your military service?

7. Who are your best friends?

8. What great selling point about you haven't I yet learned?

9. How are you planning for your retirement?

10. Are you nervous?

11. Will you take a drug test as a condition of employment?

12. Do you have any questions?

It seems to be a rule that you will always get the question that you least want to hear. At least that's what most job hunters have told me for the last 30 years. Go back over this list and identify those few that you most dislike. Prepare a positive, helpful response to each.

Tool #8: Preparing Great Questions to Ask in Your Interview

1. The job you are interviewing for:

2. The person with whom you're interviewing:

3. List key facts you have learned about:

    a. The industry:

    b. The organization:

    c. The job itself:

    d. Your interviewer:

4. Which elements of your background (school, previous jobs, special knowledge, or skills) do you think might be particularly attractive to this employer?

5. Which of your personal characteristics or qualities do you want to highlight in this interview?

6. What data do you need from inside the organization to help you decide if you would accept a job offer from them?

Based upon all of the data here, carefully construct four great questions to ask in this interview.

1.

2.

3.

4.

You may only have the opportunity to ask one or two questions. But if you have three or four great ones prepared, you have more options of what to ask, depending on what you already learned during the earlier part of the interview.

Tool #9: Preparing for Your Practice Interviews

1. Interviewer; location of interview:
2. Is your video camera ready and tested?
3. Is your resume on hand?
4. What is this job?
5. Why is it open?
6. Background of organization:
7. List of questions you want to practice (10 to 12):
8. List of questions interviewer wants to add in (6 to 8):
9. Start time:
10. Finish time:

Tool #10: Evaluating Your Practice Interview

Interviewer, jot observation notes below:

1. Opening:
   a. Handshake
   b. Facial expression/body language

    c. Was generally strong or weak

    d. Ideas for improvement

2. How tense or stressed was the candidate?

3. Any distracting verbal habits?

4. Any distracting physical habits?

5. What questions were handled well?

6. What answers need work? How?

7. Did the candidate try to uncover any potential objections? How did it come across?

8. Did the candidate succeed at overturning any potential objections? How could this effort have been improved?

9. Did the candidate use a strong close? How could it have been improved?

10. How else could this candidate have improved this interview?

Tool #11: Preparing For the Actual Interview

I.

1. Have I prepared for this interview (research and practice)?

2. Where and when is it?

3. Do I have any background on the interviewer?

4. What is this job?

5. Why is it open?

6. What is the background of organization?

7. Do I have copies of my resume and references on hand?

8. My selling points regarding this position:

9. Well-prepared questions I want to ask:

    a.

    b.

    c.

10. Trial closes I've practiced:

    a.

    b.

    c.

11. Possible objections I've prepared for:

   a. Potential objection:
      Need clarifying question?
      Response to overturn or address:
      Strong point to end on:

   b. Potential objection:
      Need clarifying question?
      Response to overturn or address:
      Strong point to end on:

   c. Potential objection:
      Need clarifying question?
      Response to overturn or address:
      Strong point to end on:

12. Here's how I'll ask for the job:

II.

I am ready with:

- A favorite outfit   Yes   No
- Clean resume copies   Yes   No
- Job references   Yes   No
- Notebook and pen   Yes   No
- Briefcase, notebook/folder   Yes   No
- Accurate, pre-tested directions to interview site   Yes   No
- Confirmed name of interviewer and time/location of interview   Yes   No

Tool #12: Job Reference Data Form

Today's date:

Name and current title:

Mailing address:

Date of first thank-you note:

Date(s) of subsequent thank-you notes:

E-mail address:

Preferred telephone number:

Best way and time to reach:

Known for how long:

From when and where:

Reference's job then:

My job then:

My strengths:

My weaknesses:

My personality:

My supervisory/management style:

Why I left:

Would I be rehired:

Fit with new position:

Career goals:

List other appropriate questions from Chapter 6.

Tool #13: Sample Job References Listing Sheet

You may be asked for your job references in person, over the phone, or by e-mail. You may be asked to actually supply a written list (like the following sample), or you may be able to give them verbally. Either way, you should have a neat, updated, accurate reference listing sheet ready to offer or to read from. If your references prefer to be contacted by e-mail, be sure to include that information.

Job References for Saul R. Tude
Paul W. Tibbets
Director
Asia Air Express
phone: (123) 456-7890
(former boss at AAE)

Grace O'Malley
President
Eire Marine Commerce, LLC
phone: (123) 456-7890
(former boss at Coastal Mutual Insurance)

Lewis B. Puller
Chairman Emeritus
International Negotiations, PLC
phone: (123) 456-7890
(former boss at I.N., PLC)

Robert Emmet
President
Pike Development Associates
Partner
phone: (123) 456-7890
peer (worked closely with Mr. Emmet at Persuasive Marketing
Tools, Inc.)

John Basilone
Owner
Superior Force Machine Tools
phone: (123) 456-7890
(former colleague at I.N., PLC)

Tool #14: Post-Interview Evaluation and Improvement

1. Date, time, location of interview; interviewer's name, title:
2. The job:
3. Was my research on target?
4. What new information did I learn about the job, the employer?
5. What question was I unprepared for?
6. What question did I stumble on?
7. What answers did the interviewer love?
8. What were the best questions I asked?
9. What questions do I wish I had asked?
10. What trial close did I use?
11. What objections did I uncover?
12. How did my "overturn/address" responses work?
13. How did I handle the issue of money?
14. Did I clearly state that I wanted the job?
15. Did I get a sense of the hiring process timeline?
16. Did I smile, keep eye contact, and use a firm handshake?
17. Did I learn something personal about the interviewer?
18. Do I have a follow-up thank-you letter ready to go?
19. What further research do I need to do before my next interview?
20. What can I do to improve my interview performance?

Tool #15: Job Offer Analysis

You should be able to answer all of the following questions before you decide if a job is right for you. Some of these questions can also guide you in your pre-interview research and help you to design useful questions to ask in the interview itself. Remember, this is *about the job itself.*

1. The job as offered:
2. How does it fit with current job target(s)?

3. Is it a unique or unusual opportunity?
4. Scope of responsibility:
5. Is it a move ahead, lateral, or down?
6. Biggest selling point:
7. Biggest drawback:
8. Assess prospective boss:
9. Assess prospective colleagues:
10. Assess prospective subordinates:
11. Others in the organization I want to work with:
12. The organization's future prospects (for example, merger, buyout, consolidation, sale):
13. Assess the organization's reputation:
14. Assess the organization's culture:
15. Opportunity for promotion:
16. Internal training/development program(s):
17. Opportunity for outside visibility:
18. Lifestyle/family issues (for example, travel, relocation, nights, weekends, overtime):
19. Who else has data I can access?
20. My gut says:
21. Issues for me to negotiate:
22. Is this the right job for me right now?

Tool #16: Compensation Package Evaluation

	Minimum	Current	Target	Current Offfer
Base salary				
Signing bonus				
Yearly bonus				
Moving or relocation costs				

Incentive plan				
Profit sharing				
Deferred compensation plan				
401(k), other matching program, or stock plan				
Pension or other retirement plan				
Sales quota, commissions, overrides, etc.				
Expense account				
Vacation				
Holidays, sick days, personal days				
Employment contract or guaranteed outplacement				
Medical insurance (individual or family plan?)				
Dental insurance (individual or family plan?)				
Life insurance				
Short-/long-term disability insurance				
Company car or car allowance				
Parking				

Public transportation allowance				
Daycare/eldercare				
Association memberships				
Club memberships				
Other				

Tool #17: Diagnostic: Is Your Job Search Stalled? (And What to Do About It)

Directions: if you answer *no* to any of questions 1–9 below, review the chapter(s) indicated to get back on track and keep moving forward.

1. Are you investing enough time and energy in your job search? (Full-time if unemployed, 10 hours weekly minimum if employed.) Review Chapters 1 and 3.

2. Are you attending to your physical and emotional health? Review Chapter 2.

3. Are you using a four-front job campaign or just using one method (for example, published openings or recruiters)? Review Chapters 3 and 4.

4. Are your job targets focused by geography, industry, and function? Review Chapters 4 and 5.

5. Are you growing your network of contacts? Review Chapters 3 and 6.

6. Are your interviewing skills improving as your job search continues? Review Chapters 4, 5, 7.

7. Are you following up with all your preliminary contacts as well as anyone with whom you've interviewed? Review Chapter 1 and 5.

8. Are you getting the number of offers you feel you should for the amount of effort you are investing? Review Chapters 7 and 8.

9. Are you able to convert a so-so offer to an acceptable offer? Review Chapter 8.

10. Are you spending a lot of time waiting for calls or e-mails to be returned, or waiting to hear back from contacts, re-cruiters, or references, or waiting for job board responses, or waiting for social media to generate job leads, or waiting to hear the results of interviews?

If you answered yes to waiting for *anything* to happen, you need to re-read the entire book because you are wasting valuable time you could be investing in productive job-hunting activities.

Tool #18: Job Search Wrap-Up

Directions: respond to the following items by circling yes or no. By taking appropriate action, convert every no to a yes before you start your new assignment.

1. I have accepted my job offer verbally
    and in writing.   Yes   No

2. I have a firm start date.   Yes   No

3. I have sent personalized thank-you/announcement
    letters to all the librarians and research assistants
    who helped me during this job hunt.   Yes   No

4. I have sent personalized thank-you/announcement
    letters to all the agencies, recruiters, and search
    consultants I contacted during this search.   Yes   No

5. I have sent personalized thank-you/announcement
    letters to everyone who actually interviewed me
    during this job hunt.   Yes   No

6. I have sent personalized thank-you/announcement
    letters to all my job references.   Yes   No

7. I have sent a thank-you/announcement letter to
    every person in my new and expanded contact
    network.   Yes   No

8. I have captured all of my relevant job-search
    expense receipts for use in my next tax return.
    (See Tool #3.)   Yes   No

9. I have completed the Research Resources Tool (#5) so I can get my next job search up to speed more quickly. Yes No

10. I have kept copies of all the letters I found useful during my job hunt. Yes No

11. I have committed to respond to every headhunter call I get in the future to build my contacts in this area. Yes No

12. I will take some definite action to ensure that my contact network continues to expand. Yes No

13. I have committed to network with any job hunter who appropriately asks for my input or assistance. Yes No

14. I have explicitly thanked my family for supporting me (okay, putting up with me) during this job search. Yes No

15. I have something planned to celebrate this significant achievement. Yes No

16. I have compiled a complete file of information, resources, contacts, and tools I have found useful in the job search. Yes No

Conclusion

This Is Your *Life* We're Talking About

I'VE PACKED THIS BOOK WITH EVERYTHING YOU NEED TO KNOW TO GET A JOB HUNT UP AND RUNNING QUICKLY, EFFICIENTLY, AND PROFESSIONALLY. I have presented a methodology of preparing for and engaging in job interviews that, if followed, will consistently put you in the first tier of job candidates. I have taught you how to close an interview on the strongest possible note, to generate more offers, and negotiate them upward more successfully. From my observations of more than 30 years in this field, I've also included how to avoid (or recover from) the costly mistakes so many job hunters make.

With insider tips and shortcuts, I've narrowed every issue down to its essential nature so that you can hit the job-hunting road in high gear and, hopefully, see some results fast. I've advised you, I've coached you, I've counseled you, and I've prodded you, but all to get you moving in the right direction. I've laid in some humor to keep you smiling while you suffer the slings and arrows of outrageous fortune that will surely come your way.

I wish that uncertainty, rejection, and anxiety were not part and parcel of the job-hunting process. But the good news is so are discovery, enthusiasm, and acceptance. If you allow yourself to focus on the potential negatives, stress and anxiety will creep into your interviews like a fog. Thus, you must train yourself to focus on each and every positive that you encounter along the way. If you do that, the fog of anxiety and stress will evaporate before your eyes in the warmth of your realistic optimism.

What I can't do, however, is go out there and do it for you. I wish I could because, if we met and after I spent some time getting to know you, I could convince almost any employer why they should hire you and no one else but you. Because I would dig and dig until I found out why they should hire you. You have that information; you are its truest source, and you must use it.

So we end up back where we started: asking the big questions. What are you looking for, why, what knowledge, skills, and experiences do you bring to the table, and what is it about you—your unique blend of personal qualities and characteristics—that will ensure your success in this new job?

A couple of folks who I've worked with through the years have fantasized about us using one of those miniature radio devices so I could listen in to their interviews and then whisper great responses into their ears for them to use. Let this book act as that device for you. Go through it from cover to cover. Ultimately, you will hear me prodding you to always out-prepare your competition. You will hear me joking with you to help you get your anxiety under control and working for, not against, you. You will hear me reassure you that you have a fail-safe answer for anything they throw at you. You will hear me tell you—even if no one else ever has—that you deserve a job you love and that it is out there if only you'll do the work to go out and find it.

I have written before and preached to thousands that I think too many of us split our lives in two—work on one side and life on the other. I have devoted my career to supporting people at work because I believe that work is too important to our hearts and souls to be cut off from life. And I believe our personal qualities and dreams are too much a part of ourselves to be checked at the office door. So often, if you love your work, you'll love your life. Certainly work is not everything, but it *is* vital to making us what we are and what we can become. So my final point is that we're not just talking about a job here; we're talking about your life.

I wish you strength, courage, and humor on this voyage. May God hold you in the palm of his hand until our paths cross again.

Index

About the Author

Dr. Paul Powers has devoted 30 years to helping others achieve career success and satisfaction. As a management psychologist, executive coach, author, and career expert, he has helped thousands of people in hundreds of companies—from CEOs to recent grads, from corporation and hospitals to and recent combat veterans—to find and succeed in jobs they love. He advises corporations worldwide on how to select, motivate, and lead fully engaged employees with executive/career coaching, management and sales team development, and pre-retirement planning.

As a popular speaker and seminar leader, Dr. Powers travels extensively, sharing his wisdom, his humor, and his deepest belief that each of us has a gift to be discovered, developed, and shared. As author of *Don't Wear Flip-Flops to Your Interview, Winning Job Interviews*, and coauthor of *Love Your Job! Loving the Job You Have, Finding a Job You Love*, Paul's energy, enthusiasm, and motivation have reached around the world to people in every imaginable field.

Dr. Powers is a licensed psychologist, the former chairman of the Massachusetts Board of Psychologists, and a member of numerous professional organizations. Paul holds a bachelor's, master's, and doctoral degree in psychology from the University of Massachusetts at Amherst. He helped found the Management Corps for the Emerging East, a non-profit initiative to send American business volunteers to work in enterprises of the republics of the former Soviet Union to assist in their transition to a free market economy with hands-on management skills and techniques. Paul is also a former U.S. Marine as well as a former licensed pipe fitter.

Dr. Powers' work has been widely noted in the media, such as the *Wall Street Journal, Boardroom Reports,* The *New York Times, National Business Employment Weekly, New England Business Magazine, Men's Health,* and hundreds of newspapers and radio stations nationwide, and he has appeared on CNN, MSNBC, WNBC, NPR, and numerous other media outlets. He co-hosted *CareerTalk,* a call-in show on a major Boston radio station.

Practicing what he preaches about the many benefits of developing varied interests, Paul also maintains a specialized forensic practice, is a voice-over artist, a screenwriter, and an avid outdoorsman, and has an active pro bono schedule both nationally and internationally. He, his wife Linda, an entrepreneur, graphic/web designer, and principal of Powers Design, and their two boxers divide their time between Florida's Gulf Coast and Cape Cod.

Sign up for a free subscription to Dr. Powers' *LifeMap* monthly newsletter, read by thousands, at *www.drpaulpowers.com.* Dr. Powers is available to speak at your organization's off-site meeting, conference, or association event with a fast-moving, practical, and engaging presentation on the many topics he covers in *LifeMap.* E-mail him at drpaul@ drpaulpowers.com.